W9-DGH-592

The Story of
Ancient Greece

ΜΟΛΩΝ ΛΑΒΕ

Fourth Edition

by

Suzanne Strauss Art

Wayside
PUBLISHING

(888) 302-2519
www.waysidepublishing.com

To David

Copyright © 2013 by Wayside Publishing

All rights reserved. No part of this publication may be reproduced, stored in a retrieval system, or transmitted in any form or by any means, electronic, mechanical, photocopying, recording, or otherwise, without the prior written permission of the publisher.

Printed in USA

6 7 8 9 10 11 KP 17

Print date: 239

Soft cover ISBN 978-1-938026-56-0
FlexText® ISBN 978-1-938026-57-7

CONTENTS

ACKNOWLEDGEMENTS

I am very grateful for the continuing support and constructive criticism offered by two of my colleagues at the Fay School: Richard Upjohn of the History Department and Daniel Arnaud of Classics. Both men are extremely knowledgeable and perceptive scholars, and they generously devoted substantial amounts of time to reading, editing and commenting upon my manuscript.

Dick and Dan, you personify the joyful spirit of inquiry that once propelled the ancient Greeks to geometrically expand their understanding of the universe and of man's place in it.

Many thanks also go to my students at Fay: They inspired me to create a series of history books that are relevant to the lives of middle school students and are fun to read. Their reactions to my sample chapters as well as their suggestions for activities helped me to produce books that are unabashedly "kid-oriented."

Most of all, much love and appreciation go to my ever-patient family—my husband Bob and my children David and Robyn. They put up with many a late dinner as I worked for "just a few more minutes" at the computer.

PROLOGUE

Twenty-four hundred years ago, a Greek statesman named Pericles delivered a dramatic speech honoring local soldiers who had recently fallen in battle and praising the city of Athens, in whose defense they had given their lives. "Future ages will wonder at us," he proclaimed, "as the present age wonders at us now."

Pericles had good reason to boast. Athens was an exceptional city—it was the birthplace of democracy and the site of the richest flowering of artistic and intellectual activity the ancient world had ever known. Try to envision the ancient cultures of the western world as a giant constellation in the dark evening sky. Among the many stars that sparkle and glisten, one is particularly brilliant. This bright star is Athens.

The fifth century B.C.E. was the golden age of ancient Greece, and, as Pericles predicted, the achievements of the Athenian scholars, artists, and statesmen who lived in those early times so impressed future ages that they have become cornerstones of modern western civilization.

But the story of ancient Greece is a long one—four thousand years long. To understand how the Athens of Pericles reached such a pinnacle in the history of civilized man, we must turn to the foundations of Greek history.

Greece's Unique Geography

Geography always has an important influence on the way a culture develops. Let's look at Greece—a mountainous peninsula in southeastern Europe stretching from the Balkans to the Mediterranean Sea. It is a relatively small region, roughly the size of New York state, but its ragged coastline is over two thousand miles long. To understand this better, take a pencil and draw a line about three inches long. Then, below it, draw a jagged line the same length, moving the pencil constantly up and down until you get to the end. As you can see, the second line would be much longer than the first if it could be pulled taut like a piece of string.

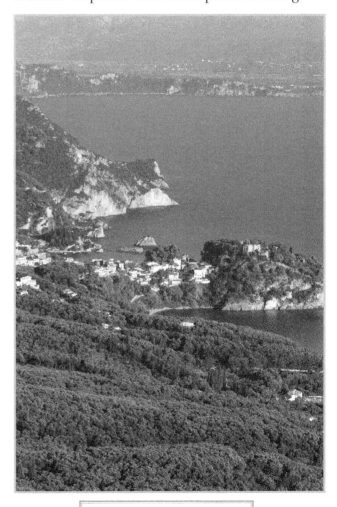

The rocky seacoast of Greece

The long Greek coastline, as jagged as the line you drew, is made up of hundreds of bays and inlets, whose quiet waters provide excellent natural harbors. Even inland areas have fairly easy access to the sea, since no part of the country is more than sixty miles from the coast. Is it any wonder that the sea has always played a key role in the lives of the Greeks?

Greece is made up of two geographical areas of approximately the same size. The southern area, called the Peloponnese, looks like a giant hand grasping at the long offshore island of Crete. (Look at the map on the previous page.) The Peloponnese is connected to the northern area of Greece by a narrow (four-mile wide) strip of land called the Isthmus of Corinth. Off the eastern coast of the northern part is a long island, Euboea.

The waters of the Mediterranean that lie to the east of Greece make up the Aegean Sea. Its calm blue-green waters are dotted with scenic islands that form stepping stones from Greece to the western projection of Asia (modern Turkey). In ancient times, this small extension of Asia was called Anatolia, a Greek word meaning "the land where the sun rises."

Rugged mountains of limestone cover over three quarters of mainland Greece. The highest one, Mt. Olympus, rises in the north 9,570 feet above sea level. The ancient Greeks believed that powerful but benevolent gods and goddesses lived on this snow-capped mountain, which is made ever more mysterious by the clouds that covered its peak. The mountains that line much of the Greek coast appear to be higher than they actually are because they plunge so steeply down to the sea. Some of the inner mountain valleys are connected by narrow passes, but most are completely surrounded by rocky cliffs. The only flat areas in Greece are along the coastal plains, in the mountain valleys, on a small plateau in the Peloponnese, and in the plains of Thessaly in the north. There are no major rivers in Greece, but mountain springs empty into cascading brooks and streams which provide a plentiful supply of fresh water.

A secluded mountain valley

Originally, the Greek landscape was heavily forested, but the ancient people cut down the trees to build houses and boats. Once the trees were gone, the fertile top soil was washed away by erosion. This explains why from very early times much of the land that was not mountainous was more suitable for the grazing of sheep and goats than the cultivation of crops.

The Greek climate is similar to that of southern California. Seasonal winds from the Mediterranean bring moderate rainfall to the peninsula during the late fall and winter months, while the summers are very hot and dry.

Today, tourists flock to Greece to admire the scenic panorama—the rugged mountains towering above the green valleys, the sparkling blue sea breaking upon the rocky shores, and the bright summer sky that makes everything appear clean and clear and crisp.

A Spirit of Independence

The early settlers of Greece built their villages in the sheltered valleys and on the coastal plains. The mountains and the sea formed imposing barriers that made travel difficult and isolated one village from another. As a result, each community had to depend upon its own resources to survive. With hard work and cooperation, the settlers were able to create a good living in a rather challenging environment.

Sometimes problems arose that affected an entire village. When this happened, the villagers gathered together to voice their opinions. The leaders listened to these opinions and then worked out a solution that benefitted everyone. The idea of ordinary people having a say in how their lives were managed was rather unique in the ancient world—in most cultures, all decisions were made by the rulers, be they kings, pharaohs, or emperors. The villagers' early experiment in self-government was a forerunner of democracy (a Greek word meaning "rule by the people"). Today, most of the governments of the world are based upon the principles of democracy that were formulated in ancient Greece.

The Greeks were a very curious people, and because they were never burdened by an oppressive, centralized government, they felt free to question and investigate anything they didn't understand. They carefully studied the natural environment and pondered the meanings of such things as the movement of stars and the life cycles of plants and animals. At first they attributed all natural occurrences to the powers of supernatural beings, but, as we will see, over the centuries their careful observation and experimentation resulted in many important discoveries in science and mathematics. The Greeks marveled at their own powers of logic and reason, and they tried to determine where man fit into the grand scheme of the universe. Their fascination with the way human beings think and act led to the creation of the scholarly disciplines of history, philosophy and psychology.

Their inquisitive spirit and a supreme confidence in their own abilities set the Greeks apart from the other peoples of the early Mediterranean world. Their celebration of what humans can do and become is reflected in the ancient statues and paintings that have been found and recovered by modern archaeologists. Their love of order and harmony is revealed in the elegant design of the crumbling remains of their buildings. Remnants of lyrical poetry and thoughtful essays written by early Greek scholars express hopes and dreams that are not so different from our own. The theater as we know it was invented by the Greeks, and many of their plays are enjoyed by modern audiences. Action-packed epics and fanciful myths dreamed up by highly imaginative Greek storytellers are still read and enjoyed probably as much as they once were so many centuries ago. They are the source of such modern metaphors as "Achilles' heel," "Pandora's box," and "the face that launched a thousand ships." As for sports, the modern Olympic Games date back to contests held every four years in Olympia, a mountain hamlet in ancient Greece.

We owe so much to the Greeks! So let's turn back the clock to those early times and look closely into the everyday lives of the men, women, and children who settled on that rocky peninsula by the sea. By learning more about them and the generations who followed them, we can gain a better understanding of our own culture. Let's begin!

Questions

1. Who was Pericles?
2. Describe the general attitude that set the Greeks apart from other peoples of the ancient Mediterranean world.
3. What is the Peloponnese?
4. What is the highest mountain in Greece?
5. Describe Greece's climate.
6. How did the mountainous terrain influence the development of self-government in Greece?

7. What are some examples of Greek culture that are readily apparent in our modern world?
8. List five adjectives that describe the ancient Greeks.

Further Thoughts

1. Our knowledge of ancient Greece comes from many sources. Archaeologists have found (and continue to find) remains and artifacts that have been buried in the ground for millennia. Many of the ancient vases that have been recovered are decorated with paintings of scenes of everyday life in Greece. Ruins of ancient buildings such as the Parthenon in Athens are still standing. Also, many Greek statues were copied by Roman sculptors, and so even when the originals are lost, the copies often have survived. Greek writers produced a great wealth of manuscripts; as with the statues, many of their writings were copied into other languages and have survived in that form.

2. *Peloponnese* is a Greek word that means "Pelops' island." According to legend, this land was once ruled by King Pelops, grandson of the god Zeus and father of King Atreus. Since the Peloponnese is connected to the mainland by only a narrow strip of land, the early people considered it a separate piece of land, an island. In 1893 a canal was cut through the isthmus, enabling "Pelop's island" to truly live up to its ancient name.

3. Even at the height of its civilization ancient Greece had a relatively small population. (There were only about 40,000 Athenian citizens.) If you examine the world map on the opposite page, Greece appears tiny and insignificant. Isn't it amazing that such a small group of people could have had

Greece's location on the world map

such a significant and long lasting effect upon western civilization?

4. Historians traditionally used the letters B.C. and A.D. to date events. Using the birth of Christ as a convenient breaking point, everything before that event, and counting backwards, was B.C. For example, twenty years before Christ was born was 20 B.C. A.D. referred to the year Christ was born. A.D. stands for Anno Domini, Latin for The Year of Our Lord. So everything after the birth of Christ was written with the letters A.D. In recent years, historians have begun replacing B.C. and A.D. with the letters B.C.E. (Before the Common Era) and C.E. (Common Era). These are the letters used in this book.

Projects

1. Make a relief map of the Greek peninsula and surrounding islands using clay or instant paper mâché. Paint the valleys and plains green, the mountains brown, and the water blue. Mt. Olympus should be painted white to indicate its snow cover.

2. Grapes and olives became the major crops of Greece. Find out how these plants are grown. What sort of soil and how much moisture do they require? Why was the natural environment of Greece so ideal for their cultivation? Write a short report.

3. Geography plays an important role in the development of any culture. The mountains of Greece fostered the isolation of communities and made them independent. Imagine that Greece had no mountains at all. Would there have been many rulers or only one? How independent would each community have been? Write a paragraph or two describing the kind of government that probably would have evolved in a country that was flat and open. (Clue: think about ancient Egypt.)

fresh green olives

Hermes, messenger of the gods

PART ONE
THE EARLY YEARS

Europe

Greece

Asia

Crete

Cyprus

Egypt

Crete lies in the eastern Mediterranean

CRETE

The story of Greece begins on Crete, a long, narrow island that lies south of Greece midway between Europe, Africa and Asia. It separates the Aegean Sea, which laps against its northern coast, from the greater expanses of the Mediterranean to the south. Crete extends 152 miles from east to west, but its widest part measures only 35 miles. It covers an area of a little over 3,000 square miles. On a map the island looks a bit like a great horned slug slowly creeping westward across a blanket of blue.

Imposing mountains tower above Crete's wide coastal plains. Snow-capped Mt. Ida rises 8,000 feet at the center of the island. The climate in the lowland areas is similar to that of mainland Greece—hot and dry in the summer, and cool and wet in the winter. Although it rains frequently in the fall and winter, the showers don't last very long. Crete is a part of modern Greece.

Early Settlers

Crete is historically important because it was the first part of Europe to be civilized, and it had a great effect upon the development of Greek culture. The island's original settlers were probably mariners from Asia, who were blown off course as they ventured westward in their small, fragile crafts across the turbulent Mediterranean Sea. When they realized that they had stumbled upon an enchanting land of gentle breezes whose soil, although rocky, was quite fertile, they decided to remain. At first they lived in caves, but later they built huts of sticks and mud-bricks. Eventually their numbers grew as they were joined by others who landed on the shores of the pleasant island.

The settlement of Crete occurred around 4000 B.C.E., during the Neolithic period. *Neolithic* is a Greek word that means "New Stone Age." It followed a more primitive time called the *Paleolithic* period ("Old Stone Age"). These terms are used by archaeologists to define the era when human beings made most of their tools and weapons from the stones they found on the ground. It was during the Neolithic period that men first turned to agriculture to supply their food needs.

The first settlers of Crete grew barley and wheat, but later generations discovered that grapevines and olive trees flourished in the island's rocky soil and temperate climate. Wine and olive oil were to become important cash crops. The settlers also herded sheep and goats for their wool and milk, raised pigs for their meat, and kept a few oxen to pull the plows that they had fashioned out

Crete

of wood and stone. They even domesticated bees for honey to sweeten their food.

The sea itself yielded a bountiful harvest of fish, which made up a substantial part of the islanders' diet. The early settlers particularly savored the taste of octopus, which they speared just off the island's rocky shores and cooked in its own ink. They cut down the local cypress trees and built small fishing boats.

The Development of Trade

As the farmers prospered and the small villages grew into towns, some of the more enterprising islanders would load their boats with produce and set sail for foreign trading ports. They brought back to Crete many new ideas and technologies as well as crafts and food products.

An early destination of these traders was the island of Cyprus which lay to the east. The people of Cyprus mined copper, a metal that could be melted down over a hot fire to make tools and weapons that were harder and sharper than the stone implements used on Crete. Once the merchant ships began bringing home supplies of the new material, Cretan craftsmen experimented with the process of melting it down and pouring it into molds. By 2500 B.C.E. they were producing fine copper daggers and spear points as well as kettles and other kitchen tools.

Trading vessels also sailed south from Crete to Egypt, where the merchants exchanged wine, olive oil, timber, wool and copper tools for beautiful stone vases. The Cretan artists used the vases as models and created their own designs of stone containers. Egypt was also the source of gold,

ivory, precious stones, faience (a type of glazed clay), ostrich plumes and linen.

Perhaps the most useful Asian import was the potter's wheel. This simple mechanism consisted of a flat stone disc that revolved within a wooden framework. A craftsman placed a lump of wet clay on the disc; then, turning the disc with one hand, he molded the clay into a perfectly symmetrical bowl or jug.

As the economy of Crete grew and flourished, more attention was given to the design of the vehicles of trade—the merchant ships. Storms in the Mediterranean can be quite violent, often occurring with very little warning, and so the Cretan shipbuilders created sturdy vessels that could endure the most blustery weather. Each ship had a very high prow that enabled it to cut through huge waves without swamping its decks, while its broad beam and deep keel made it extremely stable. These vessels were unquestionably the best afloat on the waters of the Mediterranean at that time.

The Cretan captains loved the challenge of the open sea, and their well-built ships became familiar sights at all the principal trading ports. They sailed north to the Aegean islands to barter for obsidian, a black volcanic glass that could be carved into

Major cities of ancient Crete

very sharp knife blades and spear points. Obsidian was also a favorite material for small statues. They sailed eastward to Syria where they obtained, among other objects, lapis lazuli, a beautiful blue stone used to adorn articles of jewelry. Around 2000 B.C.E. Syrian merchants introduced the Cretans to a new, man-made metal called bronze. It was formed by melting together copper and tin, and it was harder and sturdier than ordinary copper. This innovation marked the beginning of the Bronze Age in Crete. Some scholars believe that Cretan captains even ventured into the stormy Atlantic to obtain the necessary tin from the British Isles.

Pirates were always a menace in the ancient Mediterranean world. To protect their traders from attack by unfriendly parties, the Cretans built a fleet of swift armed ships. They patrolled the open seas and often escorted the merchant ships. This fleet was history's first navy.

A Powerful Kingdom

Over the centuries, Crete gradually evolved from a few coastal settlements to a vast network of over one hundred towns connected by paved roads. By 2000 B.C.E. there were three main cities on the island: Knossos, Phaestos and Mallia. Each was ruled by a king, who lived in a large palace overlooking the simple mud-brick houses of his subjects.

The civilization of Crete reached its peak of development around 1600 B.C.E. when King Minos of Knossos extended his rule over the entire island. His magnificent many-storied palace served not only as his home but also as a center for craftsmen, scribes, merchants and government officials. Some scholars believe that Phaestos and Mallia became the summer residences of Minos.

By this time, Cretan trade colonies had been established overseas in Libya, the Aegean islands, and Anatolia. By controlling the prosperous trade routes of the Mediterranean Sea, Crete had become one of the richest empires in the ancient world. Yet, when this great civilization came to an end in 1450 B.C.E. (we will find out what happened later in this chapter), it would be forgotten for thousands of years.

The Legend of the Minotaur

Until the end of the nineteenth century C.E., all that was known about ancient Crete

Theseus slays the Minotaur

came from the myths and legends created by the Greeks, who visited the island in the final years of its glory. The most famous of these stories concerned the Minotaur, a monster that was half-man and half-bull. This ferocious beast supposedly lived in an underground labyrinth or maze beneath the palace of King Minos. In Greek the word *Minotaur* means "bull of Minos."

According to the legend, King Aegeus of the Greek city of Athens killed a son of Minos in a battle that was ultimately won by the Cretans. To avenge his son's death, Minos ordered the Athenians to send a tribute of fourteen young men and maidens to Crete every nine years. (In some versions of the story it is an annual tribute.) These poor souls were locked in the labyrinth and preyed upon by the ravenous Minotaur. One year Theseus, a son of Aegeus, begged his father to send him along with the other youths on the terrible journey to Crete. The prince was

determined to destroy the monster and end the sacrifices. Aegeus protested vehemently, but at last he granted his son's wish.

When Theseus arrived on the island of Crete, he was befriended by Ariadne, the beautiful daughter of Minos. She, of course, fell instantly in love with the handsome young Athenian, and she offered him a magical ball of twine that would guide him in and out of the labyrinth. In return for her aid, Theseus was to marry the fair maiden. The bargain was made, and the prince boldly entered the labyrinth, letting the twine slowly unwind until at last he caught sight of the dreaded Minotaur. A fierce battle ensued, but Theseus triumphed, slaying the creature with a bronze dagger. His mission accomplished, he swiftly retraced his steps through the labyrinth by recoiling the twine until he arrived at the entrance where Ariadne eagerly awaited him. Wasting no time, they raced to a waiting ship. The curse was over. Athens no longer had to pay the terrible tribute.

Legends, no matter how fanciful, are nearly always based upon actual historical events. As storytellers repeatedly describe the great feats of local heroes, they add embellishments and exaggerations to heighten the drama of the tale. For example, an account of the rescue of a drowning child by an old man can, as it is told again and again, evolve into a romantic story about a beautiful princess who is saved by a hideous monster!

If this is so, what could have been the basis of the legend of the Minotaur? We know from the records of Greek writers, who lived long after the fall of Cretan civilization, that at one time Athens was controlled by the island and forced to pay tribute. Perhaps the legend of Theseus and the Minotaur grew out of a successful attempt by the Athenians to throw off the "monstrous" yoke of Cretan authority and end the tribute.

Enter Sir Arthur Evans

But there was no physical evidence that the kingdom of King Minos had ever existed, and nearly everyone considered the ruler of Crete to be a mythical figure. Toward the end of the nineteenth century, however, Sir Arthur Evans dramatically changed our perception of Crete's place in the ancient world.

Evans was a wealthy British scholar who was forced by poor health to spend much of his time in the warm climate of the Mediterranean. One day, as he was poking about in an antiquities shop in Athens, the owner showed him some small engraved stones that had been found on Crete. The stones were covered with strange, squiggly markings that appeared to Evans to be a form of ancient writing. He was intrigued, and he immediately wondered about the possibility of deciphering the markings.

He needed more samples of the curiously engraved stones, and so he sailed to Crete. Upon his arrival there he set out to explore the island villages. Imagine his excitement when he discovered that many of the peasant women who were nursing babies wore stones around their necks that were similar to the ones he had obtained in Athens. The women called the objects "milk stones" and considered them good luck charms. They refused to part with them for any price, fearing that to do so would stop their production of milk, causing their babies to starve.

So Evans decided to look for any engraved stones that might still be buried in the ground. With this goal in mind, he bought some land in the small city of Knossos where a number of ancient artifacts had already been uncovered. It seemed like a promising site. In 1894 he hired a group of local laborers and began to excavate a large mound of earth and pebbles. What he found was much more than he had bargained for!

After uncovering several bits of broken pottery, a workman's shovel suddenly struck a substantial block of stone. At first Evans thought he might have stumbled upon the outer wall of an ancient city, but further digging revealed that he had found something even more significant. The block of stone turned out to be a part of a huge and sprawling building. As his men slowly

Ruins of the palace at Knossos

The throne room

gypsum (a local grey stone that contains unique configurations of crystals), the palace radiates from a central courtyard that is 200 feet long and 85 feet wide. Facing onto the courtyard are a series of rooms that were used for official business; one contains an alabaster throne upon which King Minos himself might have sat. (It is the oldest throne ever found.) A wide stone staircase that once connected several floors of the building was originally lined with painted columns.

Light originally entered the palace through open shafts running from the roof to the ground floor. These are called light wells, and they are often used in modern buildings. Staircases and corridors led from the light wells to rooms on each level of the palace.

Evans was amazed to discover that the Minoans had modern plumbing. A system of jointed clay pipes linked the palace with

uncovered the very extensive ancient ruins, it occurred to Evans that this might be the legendary palace of King Minos! It was a gigantic structure covering nearly six acres and containing hundreds of rooms.

Evans spent the next six years excavating the remains of a great civilization, one that had been nearly forgotten for thousands of years. He named the culture Minoan after the famous king, and we will refer to it in that way from here on. Evans devoted the rest of his life to examining and even restoring sections of the historic palace. In doing so, he learned much about the lives of the people who had lived there in ancient times. He spared no expense—the total cost of his efforts was over $2 million. Fortunately, he was a very wealthy man.

The Palace of King Minos

The palace of Knossos is an extensive multi-level complex of rooms, corridors, and sweeping staircases. Constructed of blocks of

Diagram of the palace

Dolphin fresco on palace wall

a mountain stream six miles away. Each pipe segment was tapered at one end in order to fit into the next piece. Stone bridges lifted the pipeline over gullies and ravines so that the water could flow at a steady, slightly downward angle to the palace. These are the earliest known aqueducts. The system of pipes enabled the royal family to take showers and baths, and there was even a toilet that flushed when water was poured into it from a strategically placed clay pot!

The heavy rainfall in the autumn and winter months required adequate drainage in the roofs of the palace, and so the Minoan architects built an intricate system of ducts, gutters and basins on the outer walls to funnel the run-off. Some of this water was stored in tanks for drinking purposes or diverted into the plumbing system.

The design of the palace at Knossos is very asymmetrical (unbalanced). The rooms are of different sizes and shapes with hallways jutting off in all directions, and many interior walls are made up of multiple doors that could be opened to change the shape of a room. It seems that the original building was added on to in a piece-meal fashion whenever the need arose. Indeed, the entire palace seems to be a confusing, sprawling maze of rooms and corridors. Evans thought about this, and he wondered whether the legendary labyrinth of the Minotaur was actually the palace itself.

Works of Art Provide Clues to the Minoan Culture

Within the palace itself lay buried a great wealth of artistic treasures. The gold and silver jewelry, handsome stone statues and brightly painted pottery that have been unearthed reveal that the Minoans were superior craftsmen, and they also suggest that the upper classes lived in refined luxury.

The inner walls are decorated with beautiful frescoes that tell us much about everyday life on the island. Frescoes are pictures painted directly on wet plaster; as the plaster dries, the colors are absorbed and preserved within the wall surface. The Minoan artists had to work with speed before the plaster dried, and as a result their pictures seem spontaneous and full of life. Many of the paintings depict creatures of the sea: dolphins, octopi and starfish swim across blue seascapes within borders of lotus blossoms, lilies and olive sprays. The Minoan artists expressed a light-hearted enjoyment of nature, and they often took such playful liberties in their work as painting a rose

Fresco of griffin on the castle wall

Fresco of keftiu

Fragments of faience and metal objects from the Nile Valley that were buried amid the palace ruins offered proof of trade relations between Egypt and Crete. Fortunately, the Egyptians had a custom of carving the name of the reigning pharaoh upon every valuable piece of art that they made, and this helped Evans to date the artifacts.

Another fresco depicts three young acrobats engaging in an unusual sport, bull-vaulting. According to the painting, a Minoan acrobat would face a charging bull and, at the crucial moment, grab the animal's horns and then somersault onto its back. With a second somersault he catapulted from the beast into the waiting

blossom an unnatural green color or drawing a plant growing upside down!

Imaginary animals appear in many of the frescoes. The wall of the throne room is decorated with two griffins (mythical creatures that have the heads of eagles and the bodies of lions). The griffin was probably a symbol of the king's royal authority.

On another wall is a fresco of a group of tall young men with slim waists and curled black hair wearing blue and gold loincloths. Each man carries a tall conical vessel. The figures seemed strangely familiar to Evans, and then he suddenly remembered seeing paintings of similar slim-waisted youths on the walls of Egyptian tombs that had been built around 1550 B.C.E. The Egyptians had called these figures *Keftiu*, which means the "Island People" from across the Great Green Sea (their term for the Mediterranean). Archaeologists had been puzzling for years over the identity of these men whose physical appearance differed so strikingly from that of the Egyptians. Now Evans had solved another mystery—the *Keftiu* were Minoan traders.

© JEBULON / WIKIMEDIA COMMONS

Bull vaulting

arms of one of his partners. Obviously such a feat was extremely dangerous, but what was its purpose? Was the bull-vaulting simply a form of entertainment, or did it have a deeper significance? And why was the bull so important to the people of Crete? Evans thought hard and long about these questions.

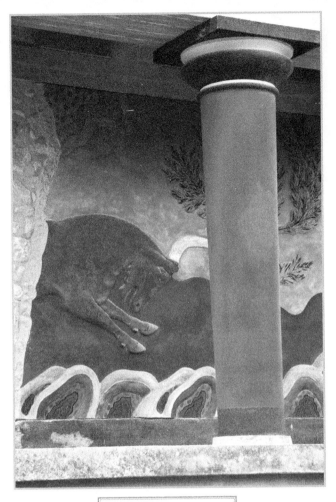

© JEBULON / WIKIMEDIA COMMONS

Close up of bull fresco

painted on the palace walls. It is likely that the double ax was another symbol of the Minoan king's authority. The Greek word for double ax is *labrys*, and so *labyrinth* means "the house of the double ax." Evans reasoned that visitors from mainland Greece must have been amazed by the great size and the sprawling design of the labyrinth. Undoubtedly they took stories back to Greece about the confusing maze of rooms and corridors that seemed to extend into infinity. If this was so, then Evans was surely correct in his suspicion that the legendary labyrinth was in fact the palace itself!

Further Clues Suggest the Power of Knossos

The excavations at Knossos revealed that the sprawling palace was rather like a self-contained village, for it contained numerous workshops and storage areas in addition to the royal living and entertainment rooms and the government conference halls. Evans' discovery of large basement vaults that were once overflowing with gold, silver, and lapis lazuli was a further testament to the great wealth of the Minoan kings. The people of Crete paid their taxes in olive oil, and huge earthenware jars (called pithoi) designed to contain that useful liquid were found in storage rooms of the lower levels of the palace. Some of these jars are as tall as a grown man.

Other palace wall paintings show young Minoan women with elaborately styled hair that is adorned with ribbons; they are wearing tight-waisted, flounced dresses and beautiful golden jewelry. Apparently an hour-glass figure was considered the ideal for Minoan men and women alike.

In one room Evans found a large bronze double ax, similar to axes that had been

But despite the great wealth of the Minoans, Evans found no sign of walls surrounding the palace. Apparently, the king's fleet of warships provided all the protection that was necessary. The Minoans must have felt very safe indeed in their island paradise, and this sense of security enabled

A double ax

Ancient pithoi

scales. To primitive people, it seemed that the snake was reborn. The snake goddess was probably worshipped as a source of fertility. The Minoans even kept tame snakes in their houses.

Religious ceremonies in Crete were most likely held in the open air, since few temples have been found on the island. Altars were built in palace courtyards and in sacred groves on hillsides and mountain tops. Offerings of food, double axes and statues of the gods were placed on the altars.

them to channel their energies into creative activities rather than defensive or destructive ones.

Other sites on Crete have been excavated since the time of Evans, and archaeologists have found the ruins of many ancient cities and palaces. However, all evidence suggests that Knossos was the center of political and economic power during the height of the Minoan civilization.

The Religion of the Minoans

The Minoans worshiped many deities, but their religion seems to have centered upon one goddess. Carved statues of a female figure holding two snakes in her hands have been uncovered at many sites. In early times, the snake was the symbol of regeneration. This is because as the snake grows it sheds its skin and emerges from it with a new set of

Carved stone horns

The services were probably conducted by priestesses. The Minoans must have believed in an afterlife, because archaeologists have unearthed tombs containing spears, cooking utensils, and clay figurines of female goddesses that were placed beside the remains of the deceased.

The Meaning of the Bulls

Surrounding the Minoan religious altars and sanctuaries were stone walls crowned with chiseled bulls' horns. Even the palace had fragments of carved stone horns on the roof, and statues of bulls have turned up in excavation sites throughout the island. Minoan traders used solid gold weights in the form of bulls' heads to determine the prices of their wares. The design of the double ax itself contains two sets of bull horns, one the mirror image of the other.

But why was the bull so important to the Minoans? The geography of Crete offers one answer. The island lies in a geographical area where earthquakes frequently occur. Indeed, the palace of Knossos was destroyed twice by earthquakes between 1900 and 1450 B.C.E. and rebuilt each time. The second time the Minoan workers reinforced the walls with wooden timbers to make them more flexible. Sir Arthur Evans was awakened one night by the sounds and movement of an earthquake. It suddenly occurred to him that the Minoans might have thought they heard the muffled roar and stamping of a bull when the earth trembled. In ancient times, people often made sacrifices to creatures that they feared in the hopes of appeasing them. It is likely that the Minoans created their cult of the bull for a similar reason. They worshiped the image of the bull and made sacrifices to its spirit in order to spare themselves the terrible destruction caused by an earthquake. Perhaps even the bull-vaulting depicted in the palace frescoes was a ritual to appease the

bull. Did the acrobats symbolize the Minoan people being tossed about on the back of an angry giant bull?

Bull statue found at Knossos

And what about the legend of the Minotaur? It is possible that on ceremonial occasions the king, as high priest of the land, wore a bull mask. The images of the sprawling labyrinth and the bull-headed man might very well have inspired the story of the monster living in a maze.

Discovery of the Minoan Writing

We learned earlier that Evans originally began excavating at Knossos in order to find fragments marked with ancient writing. Fate was with him in this search, and he uncovered many clay tablets engraved with squiggly marks similar to those he had seen on the milk stones. As he studied the tablets, he noticed that they contained more than one kind of writing. The oldest ones contained primitive picture writing, such as a drawing of a fish, bird, or plant. Other tablets

Double axes, modeled on bull horns

bore a more advanced kind of writing, a type of script.

To further complicate matters, there were two distinct kinds of script, which Evans named Linear A and Linear B. He worked for years trying to decipher the markings, but he was unsuccessful. In 1952, long after Evans had died, an architect named Michael Ventris deciphered the Linear B writing. Ventris was particularly excited to discover that the writing was an ancient form of Greek. Similar writing was also found on the mainland of Greece in Mycenae, a city we shall learn about in the next chapter. Perhaps Ventris could have eventually decoded the Linear A writing as well, but unfortunately he was killed in a car crash when he was only thirty-four. His death was a great loss for historians.

The Destruction of a Civilization

In 1450 B.C.E. the rich Minoan civilization came to an abrupt end. Sixty miles north of Crete lay the island of Santorini (called Thera by the Greeks). One day, a violent earthquake on that island set off a volcanic eruption that blew nearly everything to bits and sent a gigantic tidal wave (tsunami) over 50 feet high racing toward the shores of Crete. Hundreds of thousands of Minoans who lived on the eastern part of the island drowned. The ports were destroyed and the once invincible royal fleet was badly damaged. And there was more to come. Nearly three feet of volcanic ash gently settled over the eastern regions of the island, covering everything—cities, villages, and fields—with a soft, highly toxic blanket. Those who escaped the forces of nature fled to the western hills, where they became

simple farmers. The mighty power of the kings of Knossos was no more.

Questions

1. Describe the geography of Crete.
2. Why is Crete historically important?
3. What were the early products of Crete?
4. How do you make bronze?
5. How did Ariadne help Theseus?
6. Why did Sir Arthur Evans go to Crete?
7. Describe the palace at Knossos.
8. What is the Greek meaning of labyrinth?
9. Why did the Minoans probably worship bulls?
10. How did the Minoan civilization come to an end?

Further Thoughts

1. Recently a group of American cowboys studied the bull vaulting of Crete. They insist that the feat portrayed in the frescoes is physically impossible. First of all, they say that it is impossible to maintain one's balance while grabbing the horns of a charging bull. Secondly, it is difficult to grasp both horns because a charging bull carries its head tilted to one side. If bull vaulting is a physical impossibility, the Minoan paintings must be purely symbolic of the Minoans' desire to master their erratic natural environment ("to grab the bull by the horns").

2. A Greek scholar named Plato (more about him in a later chapter) wrote a story about an island named Atlantis that was populated by a prosperous and civilized society. One day, unexpectedly, the island

sank into the sea. Historians have been arguing for years about the existence and location of Atlantis. Many believe that Santorini was the island Plato had in mind. The eruption in the fifteenth century B.C.E. was so violent that most of the island was blasted away, leaving only the crescent shaped island that exists today. (Plato had said that Atlantis was ring-shaped.)

Baxedes
Finikia
Ammoudi • Oia
Omos
Potamos
Agrilia • Thirasia
Imerovigli
Firostefani
Fira (Thira)
Messaria
Monolithos
Agios Paraskevi
Megalohori
Athinios
Kamari
Akrotiki
Faros
Perissa
Perivolos
Agios Georgios
Vlyhada

Aegean Sea

What remains of Santorini

In the mid-twentieth century scientists found in the ashes of the remaining part of the island three-story houses that are 3500 years old. In the houses were jars filled with wine and olive oil, farm tools, and everyday implements. The walls of the houses were decorated with beautiful frescoes. The similarity between the findings here and those on Crete indicate that the houses were inhabited by Minoans. The island must have been a colony belonging to Crete. And so, whether Santorini was Atlantis or not, the island provides invaluable clues to the civilization that flourished in Crete just before the eruption of the volcano.

3. Bulls play a major role in many Greek legends about Crete. In one, Zeus (the major god of the Greeks) disguises himself as a powerful white bull and charms a beautiful young maiden named Europa. As the girl climbs onto his back, he takes to the air and together they fly to Crete. There Europa bears their son, Minos. The child grows up to become the famous king of the island.

4. Archaeologists have been aided in their efforts to establish the dates of Minoan artifacts by comparing them with similar objects made in Crete that have been found in the tombs of ancient Egypt. As we have learned, the Egyptians wrote the name of the reigning pharaoh on their valuable works of art as well as upon the walls of their tombs and temples. Egyptian time periods were based upon how long the pharaoh had ruled, so that "Rameses 21" would be the twenty-first year of the reign of Rameses. This makes it very easy to date Egyptian objects, and archaeologists can assume that Cretan artifacts buried with them were made at about the same time.

5. Some scholars believe that Minos was not the name of one specific man. Rather, it was the term given to every ruler of Knossos, like the words king or pharaoh.

Europa and the bull

6. The first person to dig up ancient artifacts near Knossos (in 1878) was a Cretan merchant named Minos Kalokairinos. Could he have been a descendant of the legendary king?

Projects

1. Theseus did not honor his promise to Ariadne. Find out what happened after the couple left Crete, and write a short report. Also, see if you can discover what happened to Aegeus when his son returned to Athens.

2. According to legend, the famous labyrinth was built for Minos by a Greek named Daedalus. Find out more about Daedalus, and discover how he and his son Icarus tried to escape from Crete. Draw a picture of their daring getaway.

3. After Sir Arthur Evans had excavated the palace at Knossos, he hired a group of artists, architects and archaeologists to help him restore certain parts of the structure to appear as they had in 1450 B.C.E. Great care was taken to make the restorations as authentic as possible, but many people feel that Evans should have left the remains of the palace as he found them. What do you think? Write a short report offering your opinion. Be sure to give reasons to back it up.

4. Make your own fresco painting. Mix plaster of Paris and scoop it onto a metal cookie sheet. Use a plastic knife to make a smooth, flat surface. When it is firm, but still damp, paint a design or picture. You must work quickly before the surface dries!

5. Many English words are derived from Greek. We learned that Neolithic means new (neo) stone (lithic). Can you think of three other English words that contain "neo"? Consult a dictionary. What do they mean? Use each in a sentence.

6. Bulls are also common symbols in modern cultures. For example, an active stock market is described as "bullish". Can you think of any other common expressions that refer to bulls? Do you know of a sports team called "the Bulls"? What characteristics does the bull symbolize? Make a poster illustrating the use of bulls in modern times.

Restored pillars at Knossos

CHAPTER 2

THE EARLY KINGDOMS

Around the year 2000 B.C.E. horsemen from central Europe began moving southward onto the Greek peninsula. They were called the Achaeans by the Greek poet Homer. Modern scholars believe that the Achaeans were but one of many groups that invaded Greece over a period of several centuries. These warriors destroyed the small villages of the primitive people who were already living there and claimed the territory for themselves. They spoke a language that was a forerunner of Greek.

Building Communities

Each tribal chieftain seized the most tillable land he could find and established a small kingdom there. On the highest promontory of his domain he built a walled fortress (called a citadel) where he and his family lived along with the soldiers and craftsmen of his clan. Most kingdoms were established on the eastern Peloponnese not far from the sea.

The common people built houses of wood and mud-bricks at the foot of the citadel and grew their crops in the surrounding area. They had to work hard to cultivate the thin, rocky soil. In fact, only one fifth of the land in Greece can be farmed at all because of the mountainous terrain. Yet, these primitive tribesmen succeeded in producing enough wheat and barley to feed their communities.

Grapes grew abundantly during the hot, dry summer and were gathered in the fall. They were placed in wooden vats and trampled by the families of the farmers

Ripening grapes on the vine

until all the juice drained out. The crimson liquid was then poured into clay pots, where it fermented into a full-bodied wine, the preferred beverage of the higher ranking people.

Groves of gnarled, broad-trunked olive trees bore large quantities of fruit. The olives were gathered and pressed to extract an

An olive grove

A herd of sheep and goats

The sheep and goats that contentedly nibbled the clumps of grass growing on the hillsides provided the early settlers with wool and milk, and they were a convenient source of meat. Powerful oxen pulled the farmers' plows. Horses were highly valued, and they were trained to draw war chariots. Using a horse for ordinary farm work would have been unthinkable.

Craftsmen produced tools and weapons for the entire community. Like the Minoans, the Greeks learned to melt copper and tin together over a hot fire to produce bronze. Tools and weapons fashioned from this orange-colored metal were significantly harder and more functional than the primitive bone, flint and copper implements they replaced.

The chieftains came to be regarded as kings, and they passed on their power to their sons. When problems arose that affected the entire community, the king met with the heads of the leading families

oil that had many uses. The early Greeks cooked with it and spread it like butter on their bread; and they burned it in clay lamps for lighting and used it as soap when they scraped themselves clean; they offered it in ritual ceremonies to their gods and sent jars of it to the citadel as payment for their taxes. They later learned to mix it with honey to produce a solution that took the stiffness out of cloth.

The Aegean Islands link Greece with Asia

to discuss possible solutions. These advisors were the nobility of the kingdom.

The Greeks enriched their diet of grain with seafood, for the Mediterranean, as we have learned, was teeming with all sorts of tasty fish. At first, the fishermen ventured cautiously into the waters of the Aegean with nets ready and spears poised. Occasionally on such outings, the mountain peak of an offshore island would come into view. Actually, the Aegean Islands are made up of the peaks of a submerged mountain range, and they are so numerous that a mariner sailing among them is never more than forty miles from some piece of land. Later generations of Greeks would settle on these scenic Islands.

The sea opened up new possibilities for trade as well as fishing for the early Greeks. Sailing a small wooden craft was infinitely easier than trudging over high mountains, and the development of a local sea trade greatly increased communication among the kingdoms lying nearest the coast. At the same time, exploration of the calm waters of the Aegean inevitably aroused the Greeks' curiosity about what lay beyond the horizon.

Common Bonds

Although the pockets of civilization scattered across the mountainous peninsula remained strongly independent, the early Greeks were united by a common language, a similar life style and a shared set of religious beliefs. Of course, they were also united by trade. The ancient religion was based on the worship of many gods. The most important deity was the sky god Zeus, but Poseidon (god of the sea) and Dionysus (god of vegetation) were also

greatly revered. The original inhabitants of the region had worshipped a female deity similar to the Minoan snake goddess, and she was incorporated into the evolving Greek religion. We'll learn more about the Greek religion in Chapter 6.

But in spite of the cultural bonds and the trade relations that had developed, fighting among neighboring kingdoms was fairly common. The early Greeks were a warlike race, and disputes over land ownership often led to bloodshed. Whenever an unfriendly army appeared on the horizon, the local farmers rushed inside the citadel walls for protection. Then the warriors drove their chariots out through the city gates to battle the intruders.

By 1700 B.C.E. southern Greece was controlled by several powerful kingdoms: Tiryns, Argos, Thebes, Pylos, Athens and Mycenae. The smaller communities were reluctant to argue with these giants, and they came to depend upon their superior might in times of war. When invaders threatened an area, the leaders of the smaller kingdoms simply appealed to their stronger neighbors to defend the local territory. As a result, a kingdom like Thebes actually controlled a very large region.

By around 1600 B.C.E. Mycenae had become the most powerful kingdom in Greece, controlling the Peloponnese as well as several offshore islands where small Greek colonies had been founded. The Myceneans established a vast commercial empire and created the first great civilization of mainland Europe. They ruled for about five hundred years, and this period is known as the Mycenean Age. You will learn all about the Myceneans in the next chapter.

The major kingdoms of early Greece

Questions

1. What is a citadel?
2. What were the uses of olive oil?
3. What factors bound all the Greeks together?
4. Who was Zeus?
5. Where was the Mycenean Empire?
6. What are the approximate dates of the Mycenean Age?

Further Thoughts

1. One reason for Mycenae's power was its prime location. The citadel overlooked a vast plain that stretched eastward to the sea. It was also close to the isthmus of Corinth (the narrow strip of land connecting the Peloponnese to northern Greece). This gave the Myceneans control of a major trade route. Any merchants wishing to enter or leave the Peloponnese had to travel through a pass near the foot of the Mycenean citadel, where they were obliged to pay a duty tax to the local officials for the privilege of continuing on their journey. The control

of such strategic locations would play an important role in the power and prosperity of Mycenae for centuries.

2. Because the early Greeks made their tools and weapons out of bronze, the period of ancient Greek history dating from 3400 until 1140 is called the Bronze Age. It ended when iron was introduced into Greece, which marked the beginning of the Iron Age.

Projects

1. The early Greeks established a system of government in their kingdoms known to us as feudalism. The king and his nobles controlled the army, and the farmers were required to pay a tribute (a tax) in the form of grain in exchange for protection against invaders. In many ways, the early citadels resembled the manors and castles of the Middle Ages. Find out more about feudalism and write a short essay.

2. We have learned that the Aegean Islands are actually the tops of submerged mountains (many are volcanoes). Find out how the Mediterranean Sea was formed and when the mountains of the Aegean were submerged in water. Write a short report.

3. Design a menu for the evening meal of a typical chieftain and his family. Think about what foods were available, and try to imagine how they would have been prepared. Be creative in your description of the various dishes. Examples: octopus simmered in wine sauce and olives stuffed with goat cheese. Don't forget dessert and beverages.

The rugged coast of Greece

CHAPTER 3

THE MYCENEAN AGE

As we know, the Minoans were skilled and experienced sailors who ruled the seas from about 2000 until 1450 B.C.E. During the early Mycenean Age the Minoan civilization was at its peak, and Crete controlled all the major trade routes and ports in the Mediterranean world.

The Myceneans had much to learn from the more sophisticated Minoans. Greek traders who sailed to Crete brought back beautiful examples of Minoan craftsmanship. Mycenean artisans at first copied the imported objects, but they soon created their own styles and designs of gold and bronze jewelry, armor, molded bowls and cups, and decorative sword and dagger handles. Since the Myceneans were an aggressive, warlike people, their art lacked the delicacy and whimsy of the gentler Minoans. Yet, the metal objects produced by the Greek craftsmen were far superior in quality to those of most other Bronze Age cultures of the Mediterranean world.

Mycenaean bronze dagger

Do you remember how the civilization of Crete was destroyed by a volcanic eruption and tsunami? When the Myceneans discovered that most of the Minoan fleet had sunk, they saw their chance to gain control of the Mediterranean trade routes. Wasting little time, they made Crete a part of their own expanding empire. They later rebuilt the damaged palace at Knossos and occupied that city for fifty years.

Mycenean merchant ships carried cargoes of olive oil, wine, sheepskins, timber, pottery and metal crafts, which they traded for a wide variety of products in the ports of the eastern Mediterranean. These overseas business transactions made the Mycenean kings very wealthy. At the same time, Greek pirates further enriched the treasuries of their home cities by looting foreign vessels. The kings used this ill-gotten booty to pay their soldiers and to acquire even more luxury items.

Discoveries of Early Greek Writing

Before their civilization was destroyed, the Minoans had introduced the Mycenean traders to the concept of writing. The Greeks adapted the Minoan writing (called Linear A by Evans) to record their own language, creating a new type of writing (known as Linear B). This is the writing that was decoded by Michael Ventris. The Mycenean conquest of Crete explains why Linear B writing was found on that island beside examples of Linear A.

In 1939 archaeologists digging at the Mycenean city of Pylos on the Greek mainland found over one thousand clay tablets containing Linear B writing. It was similar to the writing found at Knossos by Evans. The tablets turned out to be inventory lists of articles stored in a palace: "one pair of wheels bound with silver, one pair of wheels bound with bronze (unfit for use)," and so on. Also included was a list of about one hundred early professions practiced by the Minoenas, such as potter, herdsman, and shipbuilder. This data has proved extremely useful for our understanding of how Mycenean society was organized.

Mycenae Rules

With the conquest of Crete, the Myceneans gained command of a vast network of trading stations from Sicily (an island off the southwest coast of Italy) to Syria. They established a colony on the island of Cyprus in order to control the local copper supply, and they sailed to Spain for tin, the other metal required for making bronze.

The Mycenean ships were slim yet extremely seaworthy. They were propelled by as many as fifty oars. Linen sails were hoisted on thick wooden masts to catch the

wind. A large eye was often brightly painted on the bow of each ship. This was probably a symbol of good luck.

At this time, Egypt was still a great power in the eastern Mediterranean. The Egyptian empire extended from northeastern Africa to Palestine and Syria in western Asia, and Egyptian armies controlled most overland trade routes. After 1400 B.C.E., however, Egypt's power began to decline as its government grew weak and fragmented, so the Mycenean pirates stepped up attacks on Egyptian ships.

Eventually, the pirates had become such a constant threat to merchant vessels that few trading ports remained open. Seeking new

Mycenean trading centers

Troy overlooks the Hellespont

markets, the Myceneans were drawn to the newly expanding towns that bordered the Black Sea. These towns had great stores of grain that were harvested on the very fertile coastal plains, and the local merchants had established trading centers that were already bustling.

Troy

A narrow strait leads from the Mediterranean into the Black Sea. It separates Europe from Asia. This channel of water was called the Hellespont (the modern name is the Dardanelles). The entrance to the strait was an important strategic site, because whoever built a city there could control the Black Sea trade and become rich by charging fees for those ships that passed through the strait.

In the twelfth century B.C.E. the city of Troy (the Greeks called it Ilium) occupied the highly prized location bordering the strait. Troy was built on a bluff on the Asian side of the Hellespont (in modern Turkey) high above the coastal plain that bordered the sea. The Myceneans had no interest in paying tolls to the Trojans, and they relished the idea of commanding the strait themselves. So in about 1200 B.C.E. the Myceneans attacked and destroyed the city of Troy. This won them control of all the trade in the eastern Mediterranean as well as the Black Sea. It was an impressive victory, but it was to be their last.

Questions

1. What did the Myceneans learn from the Minoans?

2. How did the Mycenean kings feel about piracy?

3. Why did the Myceneans take over the island of Crete?

4. How did Mycenae become so wealthy?

5. What are Linear A and Linear B writing?

6. Why did the Mycenean traders look for new markets?

7. Why was Troy's location a strategic one?

8. What caused the Trojan War (the war between Mycenae and Troy)?

Further Thoughts

1. There is a famous Greek legend about Jason and the Golden Fleece. Jason was an adventurer who sailed his ship, the Argo, into distant waters to recover a magical golden fleece. Many scholars believe that the legend is based on the voyages of the Mycenean sailors who explored the shores of the Black Sea and brought home to Greece the gold they had obtained through trade. Others suggest that the golden fleece refers to the grain that was carried back to Greece.

2. The Myceneans used huge rocks to build the walls of their citadels. They carefully piled them in tiers without using mortar. Centuries later, the Greeks couldn't imagine how human beings ever could have lifted the massive rocks, and so they imagined that immortal giants called Cyclops constructed the (Cyclopean) walls. We will learn more about these huge creatures in Chapter 7.

Projects

1. Read the story of Jason and the Golden Fleece and present a short report about it for your class. What do you think the fleece represents?

2. Pretend that you are the captain of a Mycenean ship. How would you navigate your vessel? Remember, such basic instruments as the compass have not yet been invented, there are no accurate maps, and the boat has to be hauled up on the beach at night for the crew to eat and sleep. Write an entry in your ship's log, and draw a picture of your vessel.

3. The word Hellespont means "the Sea of Helle." Find out who Helle was and write a short report. Your best reference source is a book on Greek mythology.

4. Study the illustrations of Mycenean warriors in the books in your classroom. Then draw a picture of a Mycenean dressed for battle.

CHAPTER 4

THE DORIANS

By the middle of the twelfth century B.C.E., Mycenean civilization was in a state of decline. The constant warfare among the kingdoms weakened the strength and will of the people. And, despite the conquest of Troy, trade was not as lucrative as it had been in the days of the Minoans.

At the same time, the Myceneans were becoming increasingly alarmed by the growing numbers of uncivilized warriors who appeared on the northern borders of Greece. This ominous presence forced the Mycenean kings to focus their energies upon defense, and they began to strengthen the walls of the citadels and to stock up on weapons and food supplies. But they were not fully prepared for the destructive invasion that took place.

The Dark Ages of Greece

In about 1140 B.C.E. the Dorians, a race of horsemen even more ferocious than the Achaeans had been, swept down the Greek peninsula. They burst into the great citadels, looting or destroying everything in sight and killing the Mycenean rulers. They enslaved those people who did not manage to escape.

The Dorians were invincible because they had weapons made of iron. Indeed, their crudely wrought swords and daggers were much stronger than the handsome bronze arms of the Greeks. Furthermore, the Dorians fought with a savage brutality that startled even the Mycenean soldiers. Some of the Greeks managed to flee to the mountains of Arcadia in the central Peloponnese, where they built new villages and clung to the ways of the past. Others fled to Anatolia and established colonies there. Athens somehow escaped the onslaught of the Dorian invaders and became a haven for Mycenean refugees.

The Dorians were primitive, illiterate nomads. They had little interest in art and writing, and as a result of their conquest the written language died out completely in Greece. The invaders settled in the valleys and on the plains, particularly in the regions of Messenia, Laconia and Argolid in the Peloponnese, where they took over the fields previously farmed by the Myceneans. Eventually, many became prosperous landowners. Some became sheep herders. Since they were not great seafarers, overseas trade came to an abrupt end, although the

An iron spear head

Dorians did establish a colony on the island of Crete.

Fortunately, the Dorians adopted some of the traditions and religious beliefs of the Myceneans, and so that rich culture was not entirely snuffed out. But being fierce warriors, they worshipped only male gods. To their credit, the Dorians did bring to Greece superior tools and weapons made of iron, and although in many parts of the peninsula craftsmen continued to mold implements out of bronze, this marked Greece's entry into the Iron Age. The Dorians also ended the concept of monarchy and kingship in Greece, and local government was left in the hands of the more powerful landowners. As we will see, this was an important step toward the creation of democracy.

But despite these contributions to Greek culture, the Dorians were still rather uncouth invaders, and the years between 1100 and 800 B.C.E. were a time of general poverty and intellectual backwardness, known as the Dark Ages of ancient Greece.

Questions

1. Why was Greece in decline just before the Dorian invasion?

2. Why were the Dorians able to defeat the Greeks?

3. Where did the Greeks who escaped the Dorians finally settle?

4. What contributions did the Dorians make to Greek culture?

5. What were the Dark Ages?

Further Thoughts

1. The Dorians helped to memorialize the civilization they meant to obliterate in one important way. The fires that burned the Greek towns baked the clay tablets containing Mycenean writing (Linear B) and thus preserved them for modern historians to decipher.

2. In later years, the Dorians considered Doris, a region in central Greece, their homeland. According to Greek mythology, they were descended from Dorus, a son of a legendary figure named Hellen.

Projects

1. The Dorians learned about iron from a society in the Near East called the Hittites. Find out who these people were and write a short report.

2. Imagine how worried the Myceneans must have been about the Dorians. Write a short play about events leading up to the invasion or about its aftermath. Perform the play with some friends for your classmates.

3. The Dorians spared Athens. Why do you think this happened? Write a paragraph explaining why you think Athens was spared.

CHAPTER 5

The Rise of the City-State

For several centuries after the Dorian invasion, the inhabitants of mainland Greece remained mostly illiterate farmers who led simple lives. Yet, the sparks of creativity that had burst into flame during the Mycenean Age were never fully extinguished, and toward the end of the Dark Ages these sparks were slowly rekindled. The period of Greek history from 750 to 500 B.C.E. is known as the Archaic Age. This was a transitional era, a time when the Greeks began to look more closely at the world and their place in it, taking the first steps in a process of self-discovery that would lead to an explosion of invention and ingenuity in the Golden Age of the fifth century.

Experiments in Local Government

Early in the Archaic Age, the Greek people still lived in small, isolated villages. Each community was led by a leader who was called an *archon*, a Greek word meaning "ruler." Our word "monarch" (meaning "one ruler") comes from this ancient term. Like the kings of earlier times, the *archon* depended upon the support and advice of his best warriors.

The amount of land that could be farmed was limited in the small, rocky mountain valleys (the average valley was only twenty miles long and less than twelve miles wide), and so neighboring villages were constantly fighting with each other for possession of territory. This, of course, was nothing new in Greek history.

At first many of the villages were built on the sites of the old Mycenean citadels. But as the population of a village increased, new houses and workshops were built at the base of the hilltop. Eventually, everyone lived at the foot of the high ground, and the hilltop became the sacred setting of temples and religious shrines.

As the community continued to expand, a town and the villages and farms surrounding it were organized into a unit known as a city-state. The Greek word for city-state is *polis*. This ancient word is an important root in our vocabulary: "politician" and "police" are two modern English words derived from it. Can you think of some others?

In Athens nine *archons* ruled together. They were chosen from the most powerful and influential men in the polis. This type of government is called an *oligarchy* ("rule by the few") as opposed to a *monarchy* ("rule by one").

Another Greek word that is useful to know is *cratos* meaning "power." When the power of a community was in the hands of the social elite, it was called an "aristocracy" (which literally means "power of the best.") In modern times, the aristocrats are the "blue blood" families whose ancestors were powerful in the government and/or economy of a society.

Greek Roots in English Words

Our study of ancient Greek history will introduce us to many Greek words that frequently turn up in the English language. Below are some words (some of which you have just learned) having to do with government that are derived from Greek roots. (Greek words are in italics.)

English words derived from Greek

polis	city-state
acropolis	high city (or height of the city), site of ancient Greek temples
metropolis	the major city in a region
necropolis	city of the dead (a cemetery)
police	someone who protects the people of the city
politician	someone who works in the government of the city
politics	the art of science of running government affairs
political	relating to a government

archon	ruler
anarchy	rule by no one
matriarchy	rule by mothers or by women
monarchy	rule by one
oligarchy	rule by a few

cratos	power
aristocracy	power by "the best"
autocracy	government in which one person has unrestricted control, absolute power by one person
democracy	power by the people ("people power")
meritocracy	power or advancement based upon individual merit or achievement

Three Powerful Cities

Most Greek city-states were fairly small, having an average population of five to ten thousand people. That is about the size of a New England village. Only three city-states expanded to encompass a large area of land—these were Sparta, which ruled over the region of Laconia (and later Messenia as well), Athens, the focal point of the triangular peninsula of Attica (an area of 1,000 square miles), and Thebes, a city dominating the fertile region of Boeotia.

The Major Regions

The major regions

Elsewhere in Greece, the smaller city-states enjoyed their isolation and remained proudly independent. (The isolation offered protection, since a mountain valley could be defended fairly easily.) In these close-knit communities all the inhabitants knew one another, and the central marketplace and temple were visited by everyone on a nearly daily basis. Corinth was a *polis* whose strategic location on the narrow isthmus connecting the Peloponnese to the rest of Greece brought its people great wealth through trade. Ships bearing goods from the Aegean to the Ionian Sea and vice versa were hauled up on rollers at Corinth (later wagons were used) and pulled along a roadway across the isthmus to the Gulf of Corinth on the western shore. The Corinthians controlled this roadway (since they had built it), and they collected tolls from everyone who used it. (Does this remind you of Troy?) Because of their interest in commerce and products, Corinth was the only *polis* where craftsmen were held in higher esteem than soldiers.

Sparta was the most powerful city-state on the Peloponnese. When the Dorians first invaded the plains of Laconia, they enslaved the local Mycenean farmers, whom they called *helots* ("enslaved people"). The *helots* were forced to work the land and produce food for their overlords. Sparta was a Dorian stronghold, and as it grew, it seized new land to create additional fields for growing grain. In 735 B.C.E. Sparta conquered Messenia, a fertile region in the southwestern Peloponnese, enslaving the local inhabitants.

As it came into contact with other city-states through trade, Sparta experienced a flowering of arts and culture. Craftsmen molded fine metal objects and sculpted beautiful vases. Music was an important part of religious festivals, and poets composed lyrical verses. A Spartan bard named Alcman is often said to be the inventor of love poetry. He wrote long verses of lyric poetry, which were recited by choruses of young unmarried women.

A century later, the Messenians revolted against their rulers, and this event caused a great transformation in the structure of the government and the political philosophy of Sparta. Because it took seventeen long years to bring all the *helots* under control, the Spartans decided to take drastic steps to insure that a revolt would not happen again. Sparta became a tight military state, ever on the alert for signs of civil unrest. All trade came to a halt as the community turned inward. The Spartans became extremely conservative and avoided contact with the outside world. The protection of the Spartan way of life was considered more important than the rights of the individual, and the soldiers became the unquestioning servants of the central authorities.

In the sixth century B.C.E. the Spartans created a confederation of city-states known as the Peloponnesian League. Now every *polis* in the Peloponnese was either directly controlled by Sparta or committed to support Spartan interests in times of war.

The city of Athens had been a refuge to many of the fleeing Myceneans at the time of the Dorian invasion. During the Archaic Age, the Athenians kept alive the memory of the accomplishments of the Mycenean Age, savoring the ancient myths and legends. Although all Athenian men were expected to serve in the army, military matters never became the major preoccupation that they did in Sparta.

Surrounding Athens was the plain of Attica where farms produced large quantities of wheat, grapes and olives while sheep and goats grazed in the untilled areas. As the city expanded, the local farms could not produce enough food to support the population. So the Athenians traded their local crafts for wheat produced in other city-states. Slowly a merchant class began to grow within the community, and Athens was on its way to becoming an important trading center.

Thebes was strategically located in the center of the fertile plains of Boeotia. This region had been inhabited since the early Bronze Age, and there is archaeological evidence that Theban merchants once traded with the Minoans. The Myceneans had made settlements near Thebes, and graves from that period have been discovered containing weapons, ivory, and tablets written in Linear B. In the Archaic Age Thebes was ruled by an oligarchy of *archons*. They formed a league of Boeotian cities in the sixth century B.C.E.

Innovations from Ionia

Directly east of Greece across the blue-green waters of the Aegean Sea was Ionia, a region in central coastal Anatolia. It was named after the Ionians, a Greek tribe who settled there around the eighth century B.C.E. Although there were fertile river valleys nestled among the mountains of their new homeland, the Ionians were generally tradesmen rather than farmers. They sailed to ports around the Black Sea as well as to those on the Mediterranean Sea. They also planted many Greek colonies in places they visited.

Ionian craftsmen produced large amounts of pottery, woven cloth, and metal tools and weapons for the overseas trade. The city of Miletus was the most important Ionian seaport. In time, it would become very prosperous as an international center where people from European, African and Asian cultures mingled to trade their products and exchange new ideas.

Lydia was a kingdom lying to the east of the Ionian colonies. It was the first ancient culture to mint gold and silver coins. The Ionian merchants quickly picked up the idea of using coins instead of bartering goods, and they passed on the practice to other parts of the Mediterranean world, including Greece. Imagine the convenience of collecting a handful of coins as payment for something rather than a certain number of sacks or jugs filled with produce. The use of coinage was one of the great innovations of the ancient world.

Ionian traders came into contact with the Phoenicians, a sea-faring people living south of them on the coast of Anatolia. The Phoenicians had developed an alphabet of symbols that stood for consonant sounds. Written in combination, these "letters" represented words (the vowel sounds had to

Ruins of the ancient city of Miletus

be reasoned out and added by the reader). This was a great improvement over the cumbersome picture writing (hieroglyphs) of the Egyptians. The Ionians adapted it to record the sounds of their own language, and

Ancient coins

they improved upon it by adding symbols for vowels. By 720 B.C.E. the 24-letter Greek alphabet was in common use in Ionia, and, like the concept of coinage, it spread to the city-states of the mainland. As we learned, the Dorian invasion had brought an end to a written language (Linear A and B) in Greece. Now, with an alphabet that was easy to master, writing gradually became an essential part of everyday business transactions, and new ideas could be shared and circulated as never before. Our alphabet is based upon the one devised by the Greeks in those ancient times.

The Greek alphabet

Greek Letter	Letter Name	English Equivalent
A	alpha	A
B	beta	B
Γ	gamma	G
Δ	delta	D
E	epsilon	E (short)
Z	zeta	Z
H	eta	E (long)
θ	theta	Th
I	iota	I
K	kappa	K
Λ	lamda	L
M	mu	M
N	nu	N
Ξ	xi	XKS
O	omicron	O (short)
Π	pi	P
P	rho	R
Σ	sigma	S
T	tau	T
Υ	upsilon	U
φ	phi	Ph, F
X	khi	Kh, Ch
Ψ	psi	Ps
Ω	omega	O (long)

A Written Code of Laws

Athens, as we have learned, annually selected nine *archons* to lead the *polis*. These men chose among themselves a leader, who was called the *archon eponymos*. He was the most important man in the community. In 621 B.C.E. this lofty position was occupied by a man named Draco. He became the first legislator of ancient Greece when he created a written code of laws—the first written

Ancient Greek writing carved on Parthenon building

Solon's Reforms

In 594 B.C.E. Solon, an *archon* considerably more humane than Draco (he was also a poet), revised the Athenian code of laws. He declared that farmers who fell on hard times should no longer be imprisoned, and he removed the death penalty for all crimes except murder. He divided the Athenians into classes based upon wealth, and he set up courts with juries drawn from the ordinary people.

constitution of Athens. The laws were posted on wooden tablets throughout the *polis* so that anyone could become aware of them.

The code represented an important step in the protection of the rights of the individual. Up until then, the Athenian leaders had resolved local disputes according to their personal whims. Now they were obligated to follow an unwavering standard when deciding guilt and dealing out punishments. But Draco's laws were harsh indeed. Any debtor whose status was lower than his creditor was thrown into prison or slavery, and the death penalty was often the punishment for minor offenses, even for stealing a cabbage. It was said that his laws were written in blood. Today, the word "draconian" refers to a rule or law that has harsh penalties.

Yet, the Greeks had come a long way. Although there had been other written legal codes in the ancient world (such as Hammurabi's Code in Babylonia and the Mosaic laws of Israel), the Greek system was designed to improve the lot of the people, rather than just the ruling class.

In an important reorganization of the government, Solon created the Council of Four Hundred (also called the *Boule*). This elected body of men selected *archons* and set the agenda of items to be discussed by a larger assembly of citizens called the *Ecclesia*. Any Athenian male who had a certain income could attend the meetings of the *Ecclesia*. The poorest class (the *Thetes*), the majority of the population, were allowed to vote, but only the wealthy men could seek political office. The *Aeropagus*, a group of retired *archons* empowered to make new laws, was now opened up to members of the upper class who had not been *archons*. The *Aeropagus* eventually became a much esteemed judicial body, a sort of Supreme Court.

By restructuring the government in this way, Solon built a framework for Athenian democracy. However, despite his efforts to involve more of the people in the political process, only men owning land were involved in the assembly meetings. Women, slaves (of whom there were a great many), immigrants from other city-states, and any other non-landowners had no say at all in the local government.

Solon strengthened the Athenian economy by encouraging the export of olive oil as well as jugs and vases of glazed pottery to overseas ports. (Often the oil was transported in the jugs.) These became the chief products of Attica for centuries to come, and Athens' flourishing economy stimulated trade in other parts of Greece as well.

Political change was not limited to Athens. By the sixth century most of the Greek city-states were governed by a group of very wealthy men (an aristocracy). The most notable exceptions were Sparta and the farming region of Thessaly (in northern Greece), conservative regions that were ruled by tyrants or military tribunals.

An ancient ceramic jug

Athenian Democracy

Not long after Solon's death in 559 B.C.E., Athens was ruled by a military commander named Peisistratus who had seized power. Fortunately, he honored Solon's government reforms and the *archons* continued to hold office. He promoted religious festivals in the city and oversaw the construction of temples. He built roads and aqueducts to bring water to the city. And he created a property tax to subsidize the poorest farmers. Perhaps his greatest contribution was to build up a powerful fleet and a strong army to defend Athens against invasion. This military might would play a crucial role in the defense of the entire Greek way of life.

Government in Athens continued to evolve under the guidance of an *archon* named Cleisthenes. He divided all of Attica into small areas called *demes*, following the boundary lines of the property owned by long-established clans. Then he created ten

electoral districts, each containing a cross-section of the *demes* (each district contained parts of several *demes*). This new political make-up prevented any one district from supporting only the policies of a single clan leader. The citizens in each district voted for men to represent them in the *Boule* and at other official meetings. He expanded the size of the *Boule* and introduced an oath for

France

Spain

Black Sea

Italy

Greece

Anatolia

Mediterranean Sea

Africa

Egypt

Greece and its colonies

all those attending, in which they swore "to advise according to the laws what was best for the people."

Now all Athenian citizens had a voice in a government that was responsive to the needs of the entire *polis*, and for this reason Cleisthenes is considered the founder of Athenian democracy. However, remember that only landowners could be citizens. The wealthy continued to hold the most important administrative offices, because they were the most educated and they had the most free time. (They were the idle rich of ancient Athens.)

An Expanding Culture

By the sixth century B.C.E. there were nearly 150 city-states of varying size in mainland Greece. Overseas colonies were flourishing not only on the Aegean Islands and in Anatolia but also on the shores of the Black Sea and along the coasts of Italy, France, Spain, and northern Africa.

In mainland Greece, the geography of an area often influenced the life-styles of the local population. For example, the people living in the rolling hills of northern Boeotia raised cattle and marketed leather products. (*Boeotia* means "cow plain.") The people of Corinth grew rich through trade. They were considered loud, brash and materialistic by many other Greeks, especially the more refined Athenians. Arcadia in the central Peloponnese was a land-locked area, and its inhabitants were clannish and often culturally backwards. The farmers of Thessaly were hard-working and conservative. Ionia, a gathering place for people of many cultures, became a center for intellectuals. Athens prospered as its tradesmen brought home business profits as well as cargoes of grain from the overseas colonies—artisans from other parts of Greece flocked to the city that was rapidly becoming a center of creative activity.

Despite the isolation of many city-states and the land squabbles that frequently arose, the Greeks were united by a common language and long-established religious traditions. They looked down upon the uncivilized tribes to the north whose utterances sounded to them like the mindless "bar bar" of sheep, and they referred to anyone who did not speak Greek as a "barbarian." Pride in their common heritage and love for their homeland nourished a sense of patriotism among the Greek people that was to prove an important advantage against foreign invaders.

Questions

1. What is an archon?
2. What is an acropolis?
3. What city-state cared the most about military matters, and why did it do so?
4. How did Athens deal with the problem of a food shortage?
5. How did the Greeks improve upon the alphabet of the Phoenicians?
6. Why does "draconian" mean harsh?
7. How did Solon improve the Athenian government?
8. Why is Cleisthenes considered the founder of Athenian democracy?
9. What bonds held all Greeks together?
10. What is the derivation of the word "barbarian?"

Further Thoughts

1. The ancient Greeks called themselves the Hellenes (the descendants of a legendary hero called Hellen). Today the Greeks call their country Hellas, and specific periods of Greek history are referred to as Hellenic and Hellenistic. Why, then, do we call them the Greeks? The name goes back to a colony in Italy founded by people coming from the Greek village of Graica. The colonists were called the Graii which was translated as Graeci in Latin, the language of the Romans. In English Graeci becomes "Greek". This term was applied to all people coming from Greece. To be accurate, we should be speaking of the Hellenes, not the Greeks, but it is difficult to change a tradition carried on by historians for over two thousand years.

2. Although Alcman's poetry was written down in six books, they were lost during the Middle Ages. The poet was not forgotten, though, as his name appeared in the writings of later Greek authors. But everything changed in the mid-nineteenth century with the discovery of a papyrus near the tomb of the second Great Pyramid in Egypt. It contained 100 verses of a song performed by a chorus of young women. A century later, more papyrus fragments bearing his verses were discovered in a dig at an ancient Egyptian garbage dump!

3. Peisistratus seized power in an ingenious way. He slashed his body with a knife and gashed the sides of the mules hitched to a wagon. Then he drove the mules into the Athenian marketplace and shouted that he had been attacked by

political enemies. The assembly immediately voted to give him a bodyguard. He then used the guard to attack the city, crush the government, and declare himself ruler. On another occasion, in an effort to regain the power he had lost, he arranged to have a large woman dressed in gold armor driven in a chariot into Athens. Claiming to be the goddess Athena, she ordered, "trust Peisistratus." The people accepted her advice, and he regained power.

4.   As with our alphabet, the Greek letters have upper and lower case forms. See the chart below.

5.   A variety of sweet seedless grapes was grown on the hillsides of Corinth. They are the source of our modern "currants".

Projects

1.   Here is a game the class can play. Study the chart showing the Greek alphabet on page 42. Divide into two teams. Each team should have a copy of the Greek alphabet. The teacher writes a short message using the Greek letters and gives a copy to each team. The first team to translate the message wins. Now try another message.

2.   It has been said that Draco's laws were written in blood, not ink. Explain what this means.

3.   One out of every ten English words comes from the Greek language. We have learned about some that have to do with government. Some other examples are amnesia, catastrophe, enigma, choir, chorus, agony, apology, school, orchestra, pentathlon, and thesis.

Α Β Γ Δ Ε Ζ Η Θ
Ι Κ Λ Μ Ν Ξ Ο Π
Ρ Σ Τ Υ Φ Χ Ψ Ω

α β γ δ ε ζ η θ
ι κ λ μ ν ξ ο π ρ
ς σ τ υ φ χ ψ ω

Upper and lower case Greek letters

4. Below are some Greek word roots, prefixes, and suffixes—and their meanings. By combining them, you can form English words. Here are some examples: *bio* (life) + *graph* (something written) = biography (a written account of a life); *hippo* (horse) + *potams* (river) = hippopotamus (literally, a river horse). How many words can you make?

Greek Roots and definitions

Greek root	Meaning
Anthropos	man, human
Arachne	spider
Archaeo	ancient
Biblios	book
Bios	life, living things
Chrono	time
Crypto	hide, or hidden
Cyclo	wheel
Dromos	racecourse or arena
Gon	figure having angles
Grapho	to write
Hippo	horse
Logos	word of study
Pathos	feeling, suffering
Philos	loving of
Potamo	river
Psycho	mind, soul
Rhinos	nose
Sophia	knowledge, wisdom
Sphero	a round object
Theos	god
Zelo	ardent feeling

Greek prefix	Meaning
Anti-	against
Auto-	self
Geo-	earth or of the earth
Hemi-	half
Hyper-	excessive or excessively
Mega-	large
Micro-	small
Mono-	single
Neo-	new, recent
Pan-	all
Poly-	many
Tele-	far, distant
Thermo-	warm
Tri-	three

Greek suffix	Meaning
-gram	something written or drawn
-graph	something written, or an instrument for writing
-log	speech, discourse
-logy	study of something
-meter	measure, or measuring device
-phobe	fear of something
-phone	sound, device that receives or emits sound

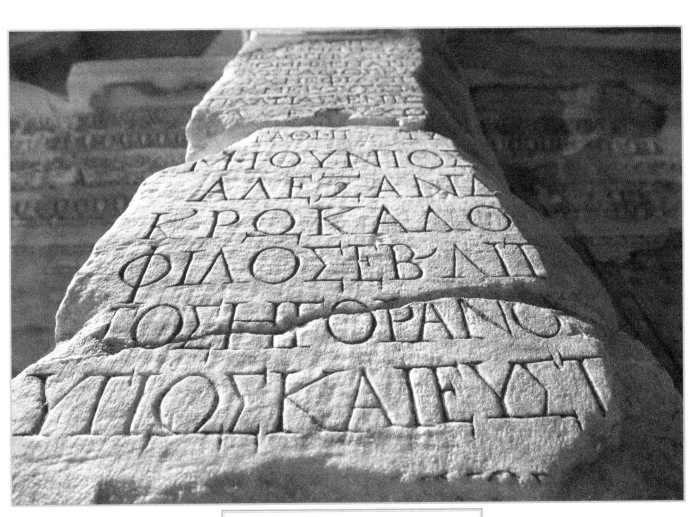

Greek letters on an ancient ruin in Ephesus

PART TWO
MYTHS AND LEGENDS

CHAPTER 6

THE GREEK RELIGION

The early Greeks did not understand why changes occurred in their natural environment, so they attributed such happenings as a sudden thunderstorm or the ever-changing tides of the sea to the powers of divine spirits. From the times of the Achaeans, every town and village worshipped its own local deities, such as the god of the eastern meadow or the goddess of the mountain stream. There were, in fact, hundreds of deities, each one controlling some aspect of nature. The Greeks also wondered about their own species—why did people suffer? why did they die? what happened to them after they stopped breathing? They concluded that, like the natural world around them, their own destinies were controlled by invisible spirits.

Over the years, storytellers made up a collection of tales, called myths, about the activities of the mysterious, unseen beings that seemed to control their lives. These myths formed the core of the Greek religion. They provided popular entertainment while they explained how the world got to be the way it was. The people loved to hear these fanciful tales, and their belief in the powers of the gods made them less anxious about the forces of nature. If they could not control a bolt of lightning, at least they could understand why it happened.

Hesiod

Every generation contributed new stories as more questions arose that needed to be answered. Before long, there were so many

deities, often competing for the same powers, that there was a great need to organize them. There gradually evolved a loose hierarchy of gods and goddesses—most of them with human-like form—who were believed to be responsible for the creation and the functioning of the earth and its inhabitants. The myths about these deities were passed down from generation to generation by word of mouth until the advent of writing.

Hesiod was a Boeotian poet of the eighth century B.C.E. He wrote a long religious poem entitled *Theogony* that drew together many of the circulating myths of his time, presented the genealogy of the gods (their family tree) and offered the Greek version of the creation of the earth. Most writers who came later used the works of Hesiod as a primary source. (The other primary source was the works of Homer, who you'll meet in the next chapter.)

The Creation

A common knowledge of the mythology united all the people living in the widely scattered Greek city-states on the mainland and abroad. Here are some stories about the origins of the gods, according to Hesiod, and the first generations who ruled the earth.

In the beginning, the Greeks believed, before there was a world as we know it, there was only confusion (Chaos). Out of Chaos sprang Mother Earth (Gaea, or Gaia) and the sky (Uranus). A huge, tempestuous sea (Ocean) encircled Gaea. Applying this information to their rather sparse knowledge of geography, the ancient Greeks reasoned that southern Europe, western Asia and northern Africa (which they considered a part of Asia) made up the land areas of the earth, and that this land was surrounded by a vast and infinite body of water. They assumed that the entire earth was a flat disc, topped by the solid dome of heaven. Below the surface of the earth lay the Underworld.

Gaea had created all the plants and Uranus provided them with life-giving rain. The water filled the lakes and rivers. Then Gaea and Uranus created the animals, as well as a variety of nymphs, fauns, and other nature spirits.

The Titans

The children of Gaea and Uranus were called the Titans. There were twelve of them, including Hyperion (the sun god) and Phoebe (goddess of the moon). The most powerful Titan was Cronus. Gaea and Uranus also produced some terrible monsters called the Cyclops, huge one-eyed creatures (their name means "wheel-eyed").

Later, Gaea was greatly angered when Uranus cast the ugly Cyclops down to Tartus, a deep and gloomy pit in the Underworld. Seeking revenge for this crime against her offspring, she persuaded Cronus to attack his father with her sharp flint sickle. When he did so, drops of the blood of the wounded sky god turned into fearsome-looking Giants (they would be enemies of the later gods) and the three bat-winged Eumenides (the avengers of the unpunished sins of men). You might know the Eumenides by their Roman name, the Furies. Uranus was then banished by his son. But before departing, he

predicted that, some day, Cronus, too, would be deposed by one of his own children.

Following the departure of Uranus, Cronus became the king of the Titans, and his sister Rhea became his wife. But Cronus could not forget his father's terrible prophecy. In a determined effort to protect his reign, he snatched up each of the five babies that Rhea bore him and swallowed it. Rhea was horrified, and when she became pregnant for the sixth time, she secretly went to Mount Lycaeum in central Greece to bear her child. After the birth Cronus asked to see the baby. Rhea cleverly wrapped a stone in some blankets and presented it to her husband—believing that the bundle was his child, Cronus promptly swallowed the stone. As for the baby (a boy named Zeus), he was secretly whisked off to Mt. Ida in Crete to be raised by nymphs and a magical goat named Amaltheia who fed him through her horns.

Zeus grew into splendid manhood, and his mother dreamed of the day he would become king. Since Cronus had never seen his son, it was easy for Rhea to introduce Zeus into the divine court as a royal cup-

Ancient sculpture of Zeus

bearer. This role enabled him to prepare a noxious potion and to serve it to Cronus in his golden cup. The drink made the king violently ill, and he spat out all five of the children he had swallowed: the goddesses Hestia, Demeter and Hera and the gods Poseidon and Hades. Since they were supernatural beings, they were quite unharmed (and fully grown).

Then Zeus and his brothers (Poseidon and Hades) attacked their father and drove him off. Uranus' terrible prophecy had come true! Afterwards, the brothers liberated the Cyclops from Tartus. In gratitude for their freedom these rather hideous creatures made thunderbolts for Zeus, a forked trident for Poseidon, and a magical helmet for Hades that would render him invisible. The thunderbolts helped Zeus to subdue the other Titans and rise to the pinnacle of divine power.

The Olympians

The three brothers divided up Cronus's kingdom: Poseidon became the god of the sea, Hades (also known as Pluto) was to rule the the land of the dead (a part of the Underworld), and Zeus assumed command of the heavens as well as supreme authority over all the gods and goddesses. Demeter became the goddess of the harvest, Hestia the goddess of the hearth, and Hera the goddess of women and of childbirth.

Zeus and his siblings resided in a majestic bronze-floored palace on Mount Olympus. This is the tallest mountain in Greece, rising nearly 10,000 feet into the heavens near the coast of Thessaly. Its snow-capped, cloud-covered peak creates an aura of mystery, and for the early Greeks it seemed the perfect dwelling place for their gods.

Zeus had many children, born to his wife (and sister) Hera as well as to his numerous other loves. His most important offspring

Mount Olympus

were Apollo (the god of music, health, and prophecy), Artemis (goddess of the hunt), Ares (the god of war), and Hephaestus (the god of metal working). Athena (goddess of wisdom and of combat) was born to Zeus' wife Metis in a most unusual way. Having heard a prophecy that any child of his born to Metis would become greater than himself, Zeus changed the pregnant Metis into a fly and promptly swallowed her. But he soon developed a terrible headache, and he begged Hephaestus to split his skull open with an anvil in order to lessen the pressure. Zeus's suffering ended abruptly when Athena sprang from his head—fully grown and fully armed. He had nothing to fear from this child, since she was born to *him* and not Metis! Another Olympian was Aphrodite, the goddess of love, who burst into life from the foam of the sea (*aphros* is the Greek word for foam). Some myths suggest that she sprang to life from the blood of Uranus. Altogether there were twelve major gods and goddesses dwelling on Mt. Olympus.

Statue of Athena

The Olympians

ZEUS, god of the heavens and king of all the gods. His symbol was the thunderbolt. Sacred to him were the eagle and the oak tree.

ZEUS

HERA, wife of Zeus and protectress of wives and mothers. Her symbols were the pomegranate, the cow and the peacock.

POSEIDON, god of the sea. His symbols were the forked trident, the dolphin and the horse (he gave the first horse to man).

HERA

POSEIDON

ATHENA, goddess of wisdom, reason and purity, protectress of civilized life. A warrior, she was Zeus's favorite child (she carried her father's breastplate called the aegis). Her symbols were the owl and the olive tree.

ATHENA

DEMETER, goddess of the harvest and of fertility. Her symbol was the sheaf of wheat.

HESTIA, guardian of the hearth, domesticity, and family. She chose no symbol for herself.

APOLLO, god of music, light, health and prophecy, he was the son of Zeus and Leta. His symbols were the lyre and the laurel tree. He was also identified with the sun.

APOLLO

ARTEMIS, goddess of the hunt (and twin sister of Apollo). Her symbols were the cypress tree, the moon, the deer, and the hunting dog.

ARTEMIS

APHRODITE, goddess of love and beauty. Her symbols were the rose, the myrtle tree, the dove, the sparrow, and the dolphin.

APHRODITE

ARES, god of war. A bloodthirsty fellow, his symbol was the vulture.

HERMES, Zeus's messenger and god of thieves, business and mischief. The son of Zeus and Maia, he was cunning and shrewd. He wore a winged hat and winged sandals and carried a cadeusus (a staff entwined with two olive branches—later two snakes—and capped with a set of wings). Today the cadeusus is the symbol of medicine.

HERMES

HEPHAESTUS, god of metalworking and smiths, and patron of crafts. His symbol was a hammer.

HADES (Pluto), god of the Underworld and land of the dead. An important god, although he did not live on Mt. Olympus.

DIONYSUS, god of wine. His symbol was a cluster of grapes. He later replaced Hestia on Mt Olympus.

DIONYSUS

The Greeks imagined that the family of Olympian gods resembled those of their own leaders. Since in earliest times they were ruled by kings, they envisioned Zeus as a powerful monarch. And just as the king and his family and noblemen originally lived in a citadel on an acropolis high above the houses and fields of the ordinary people, so, too, did Zeus live in a beautiful palace atop the highest mountain in Greece.

Statue of Poseidon

Greek society is reflected by the Olympians in other ways as well. For example, Greek leaders often enjoyed the company of more than one woman. Zeus had several wives as well as numerous girlfriends. Greek women did not have the freedom to do anything about their husbands' extra-marital activities, and Hera was continually angered and frustrated by Zeus's carryings-on.

Nearly all the Olympian gods were very handsome and the goddesses were beautiful. The exception was Hephaestus, who was ugly and lame. Zeus arranged for him to be married to Aphrodite, the goddess of love and beauty, much to her displeasure. A magic fluid called *ichor* flowed through the veins of the deities, and they dined on nectar

Godlike Heroes

Apart from the colorful myths told about the Olympian gods and goddesses, there were also many popular legends about heroes who were their offspring. The greatest of the Greek heroes is Heracles (his Roman name is Hercules), the son of Zeus and a mortal woman, Alcmene. He had extraordinary strength, courage, and ingenuity, although he was not always wise. He did use his wits (and strength) to perform ten great labors, such as killing the ferocious Nemean lion, capturing the Minoan bull, battling Cerberus, the three-headed dog, and cleaning the stables of a herd of gigantic horses. Heracles

Statue of Aphrodite

and ambrosia (this divine food and drink made them immortal). Yet, the gods were far from perfect beings, as we have seen with Zeus. They often exhibited such unpleasant human weaknesses as pride, envy, and even dishonesty.

Life could be dull on Mt. Olympus, and so the gods often amused themselves by manipulating the everyday lives of the mortal humans who lived on the earth below. They could disguise themselves as practically anything—an old beggar, a young child, or even a bird—and suddenly appear among ordinary people. Sometimes they even fell in love with human beings and had children with them, producing offspring that were half-human and half-god (such half-breeds were not immortal).

Heracles wearing the skin of the Nemean Lion

was the only man born of mortal woman to become a god upon his death.

We've already learned about the hero Theseus, who killed the Minotaur of Crete (see Chapter 1). There were many others. Jason, set out on a quest for the miraculous Golden Fleece. He led a group of warriors known as the Argonauts. Cadmus fought a legendary dragon. When he killed it, he planted its teeth in the soil, then watched an army of warriors spring up from them. Bellerophon rode a winged horse named Pegasus. He slew the Chimera monster and later tried to ride Pegasus to Mt. Olympus. (This was a big mistake!). Atlanta was a heroine who sailed with the Argonauts. She was a great runner, but she lost an important race when her competitor kept diverting her by dropping the Golden Apples of the Hesperides at her feet.

These are just a few of the colorful characters the ancient Greeks loved to hear about. They are still popular today, often appearing in movies, video games, and other popular media. And, of course, stories about them and the Olympian gods remain a rich part of the literature of the western world.

Prayers and Sacrifices

Believing that the universe was controlled by the gods, the Greeks reasoned that a deity would help a human who pleased him (or her) or inflict pain and suffering upon someone who angered him. Convinced that their very lives were in the hands of the gods, the Greeks worshipped the Olympians constantly, offering prayers to the appropriate deities before they did anything important. For example, they prayed to Poseidon for a safe sea voyage,

Pegasus

to Ares for success in battle, to Demeter for a good harvest, and to Dionysus for a full-bodied wine. When something went wrong, they assumed that one of the gods had been offended, and they hastened to offer an effusive prayer begging forgiveness.

The Greeks even sacrificed animals to please the gods. After a sacrificial goat or ox was slaughtered, its entrails (internal organs) were often removed and examined by priests who specialized in this procedure. The Greeks were very superstitious, and they believed that such natural maladies as a bloated goat liver predicted bad times for the community, while a bright color detected in newly retrieved intestines was a good omen. Once the organs had been examined, the slaughtered animal was roasted over a fire. The thigh bones were wrapped in fat and burned as an offering to the god, but the rest was eagerly consumed by the worshipers. Actually, religious ceremonies were among the few occasions when meat was eaten by the Greeks, whose typical meal consisted of bread, fruit, vegetables and cheese. You will learn more about their diet in Chapter 13.

Every city had its own patron deity and local gods in addition to the Olympians, and altars were set up in homes and public places. Food and wine were traditionally offered to the neighborhood spirits at every meal. Annual festivals held to honor the patron gods provided the people with an opportunity for merry-making and feasting after the conclusion of traditional processions and sacrifices. In these local festivals lay the origins of Greek theater and the Olympic Games, which we will study in depth in later chapters.

Every town had a public hearth dedicated to the goddess Hestia. When a city-state founded a new colony, it sent fire from its official hearth to ignite a new hearth in the colony. This tradition symbolized the kinship between the old and new communities. The fire was probably transported via a large

Statue of Apollo

smoldering log that was packed in hot coals and placed in a metal container. In the same spirit of kinship, a new bride always carried a burning log from her family hearth to light the fire in her new home.

The religion that evolved in Greece was closely tied to the daily lives of the people, and its mythology as well as its rituals and ceremonies created a rich heritage. Yet, there was something missing: a moral code of behavior. As we have seen, the gods often acted in an immoral manner. Nor was there an earthly reward for virtue. The Greeks seem to have shrugged off every imaginable character weakness but one: excessive pride or arrogance (*hubris*). However, they did frown upon anyone who broke an oath or failed to honor the local gods. But given the lack of moral guidelines or spiritual appeal, many historians describe the Greek religion as little more than ceremonial bargaining with supernatural powers to obtain special favors. Still, there were those wonderful stories.

There were few priests, since religious festivals and sacrifices were usually conducted by state officials. The principal duties of the priests were to look after the temples and to assist at services held there. At such private occasions as the birth of a child or a marriage, the head of the household led his family and friends in prayer.

A Greek temple was a simple rectangular stone structure with a pitched roof that was supported by pillars. Inside was a sanctuary containing a statue of a particular god or goddess. The building itself was considered the home of the deity rather than a place of worship. Religious ceremonies took place at an outside altar near the temple's entrance.

The Greek Concept of Death

When a Greek person died, the woman of the household washed the body and anointed it with olive oil, dressed it in white, and then placed a wreath upon its head. A funeral procession of mourners and flute players accompanied the body to its final resting place. A man was buried with such personal possessions as a spear, a shield, and farming tools. Women were often buried wearing their favorite pieces of jewelry and surrounded by cooking pots.

The Greeks believed that after death a person's soul went to the land of the dead in the Underworld. To get there, it was first guided by Hermes to the banks of the River Styx. There a coin was given to Charon, the ferry-man, to gain passage across the water (for this reason, a coin was always placed in the mouth of the dead body just before burial). On the other side of the Styx waited Cerberus, a three-headed dog whose duty was to stop the living from entering the Underworld and to prevent the dead from escaping. Once past Cerberus, the soul drank from the waters of another river, the Lethe—this caused it to forget about life on earth. When a person loses interest in

Heracles battling Cerberus

life, he becomes tired and bored; the word "lethargy" is derived from Lethe. So is the word "lethal."

Next came a judgment of the quality of the deceased person's former life. The souls of wicked people were sent to Tartarus, the gloomy part of the Underworld where they were subjected to eternal discomfort. Most people ended up in the Asphodel Fields, a grey, boring region where they drifted about aimlessly in the shade, waiting for a living person to offer them a sacrifice (simply to break the monotony). Truly virtuous people went to the Elysian Fields to live in golden sunlight forever. The soul of a virtuous person could be born again, and if it gained entry to the Elysian Fields three times it could advance to the Isles of the Blessed and share eternal happiness with Cronus and many other deities in a heavenly paradise. Admission to this lofty realm was nearly impossible, but it provided a certain incentive to the Greeks to live virtuous lives.

The Oracles

Throughout Greece there were many religious shrines called oracles where ordinary people could ask questions about the future. Special priests at these shrines passed on the messages to the gods and then interpreted the divine responses.

There were over 250 oracles in Greece, but the most famous one was Apollo's temple at Delphi. This shrine was built on the slope of Mt. Parnassus, a rugged ridge rising 8,000 feet just north of the Gulf of Corinth. It was a most dramatic setting, and the Greeks considered it the center of the world. There, in an underground chamber connected with the shrine, a priestess called the Pythia sat upon a golden stool. She breathed in vapors that rose up from a vent in the floor, frequently nibbling on laurel leaves at the same time. The vapors put her into a trance, during which she supposedly communicated directly with the god Apollo.

A visitor to Delphi was expected to sacrifice a goat outside the temple before entering the shrine. He then wrote down his question and gave it to the priests. They, in turn, posed the question to the Pythia. As she ranted and raved, they copied down her incoherent mutterings as best they could. Then they translated the "message from Apollo" into a rhymed prophecy and presented it to the visitor.

Military leaders and high-ranking government officials often came to the temple for advice before taking important actions, while common people asked more mundane questions, such as when to plant the next crop or whom to marry.

As you can imagine, it was difficult for the priests to figure out the meaning of a message. They knew that their oracle would lose its good reputation if they made inaccurate predictions, so they gave answers that had double meanings. For example, when an Athenian general asked how to defend his city, the oracle advised seeking protection behind "wooden walls." But what were the wooden walls? Were they the walls of the city or the walls of a ship? We will discover which was the best answer in a later chapter.

Actually, the constant stream of visitors to Delphi taught the priests much of "world affairs," and they became very knowledgeable. As a result, their advice tended to be better than you might expect. In 363 C.E. the Pythia announced that she would give no more predictions. And she was right! Soon afterwards the temple was ransacked by the Romans, and it gradually fell in ruins.

Some Greek oracles used rather imaginative methods to predict the future, methods about as accurate as reading the tea leaves at the bottom of a cup. For example, at one oracle a man's fate depended upon whether a goat shook its head or simply stood quietly. The oldest oracle was Dodona in Epirus, a stormy and mountainous region in northwestern Greece. This was a temple of Zeus, and the divine messages were issued from a sacred oak tree. The priests wrote the words on individual leaves, and these were carried by the wind to the person who had posed a question. At an oracle in Thessaly, the visitor put a coin on the altar and burned incense. Then he put his fingers in his ears and ran off. At a certain distance from the shrine he removed his fingers from his ears. The first thing he heard anyone say about anything was supposed to be the answer to his question.

Ruins of the Temple of Delphi

Religion and Science

Their belief in the deities of Mt. Olympus did not prevent the Greeks from further exploring and questioning the order of the natural world. They saw no contradiction between religion and science, for they felt that by studying nature they were drawing closer to the divine powers that controlled everything. It was not until fairly late in the civilization of ancient Greece that many people began to question the existence of the Olympians.

Artemis, goddess of the hunt

Questions

1. According to the myths, who were the first Greek gods?
2. What prophecy worried Cronus?
3. How did Rhea protect Zeus?
4. How did Zeus and his two brothers divide up their father's kingdom?
5. In what ways were the gods and goddesses less than perfect?
6. Who was Hesiod and why is he important?
7. Who was Cerberus?
8. What were the Elysian Fields?
9. How did the priests at the oracles solve the problem of finding acceptable answers to difficult questions?
10. How did the Greeks reconcile their religious beliefs with their respect for human reasoning?

Further Thoughts

1. The Greeks created a democratic society in which the individual had a say in how his life was governed. They had a positive attitude about the human potential, and so it is not surprising that their religion was based upon human-like deities. By thinking of their gods as being somewhat like themselves, only better, were they not also dreaming of the heights that they, as human beings, might attain?

2. Croesus, the king of Lydia in Asia Minor, once consulted the Oracle of Delphi to inquire whether he would win the war he was fighting. He was told that a great army would be destroyed. The king assumed that this meant that he would conquer his enemy.

Unfortunately for him, it was his own army that was destroyed!

3. Tartarus was a horrible place of eternal punishment. The Tartars were a Mongolian tribe led by Genghis Khan in the twelfth century C.E. Their bloody and violent invasion of central Asia made that part of the earth seem as unpleasant a place as Tartarus was said to be. The similarity of these two words (Tartarus and tartar) that refer to something terrible is an interesting coincidence.

4. Deities that are believed to have a human shape are called anthropomorphic (a Greek word that means "assuming human form"). Belief in more than one god is called polytheism (a Greek word that means "many gods").

5. Gaea's name forms a root in the words geology and geography, sciences related to the makeup of the earth's surface.

Projects

1. There are many excellent books containing the Greek myths. Find one and read as many of the myths as you can. You will probably want to read them all. *D'Aulaires' Book of Greek Myths* is a classic and a good place to begin.

2. Learn more about the creation of the world according to the religion of the early Greeks. Then draw a family tree, showing the relationships of the most important gods and goddesses.

3. According to an ancient myth, there was once a serpent called the Python that lived in a cave on Mt. Parnassus. It was slain by Apollo. The Pythia's name is derived from

it. Find out more about the story and make a short report to the class.

4. Carved into the stone at the Oracle of Delphi are two famous expressions: "Know Thyself" and "Nothing In Excess." Choose one of the expressions and write a paragraph or two about what you think it means. Try to imagine yourself in ancient Greece as you consider the meaning.

5. Tantalus was the father of Pelops (remember Pelops' Island?). He was favored by the gods, and one night he invited some of them to dinner. He wanted to impress his immortal guests with a meal that was quite out of the ordinary. Find out what he served. Why were the gods so offended by his choice? How was he punished? What does the word "tantalize" mean?

6. This is a group project. Write a play based on one of the myths you have read. Feel free to modernize the expressions and the setting. Then present it to your class.

7. In ancient Greece cosmos meant order and harmony, the opposite of chaos. Today, cosmos refers to the universe (which the Greeks considered to be orderly), and cosmopolitan means "citizen of the world"

(someone not restricted by local prejudices). Explain the meanings and derivations of these adjectives: gigantic, titanic, chaotic, and geometric. Use them in sentences. Can you think of any other words that come from Greek mythology?

8. Medusa was a Gorgon. She had snakes instead of hair, and if you looked at her, you were turned to stone. A hero named Perseus figured out a way to behead her. He then used her head as a defense weapon until he gave it to Athena to place on her shield. Look in some books or online to discover how Perseus defeated the ugly monster.

9. The Birth of Venus is a famous painting by Renaissance artist Botticelli. It depicts Aphrodite (Venus is her Roman name) standing in a giant seashell at the moment of her "birth." Painters of the Renaissance were very interested in the mythology of ancient Greece and Rome. Find the painting in an art book or online. Read the commentary about it.

Athena's shield

Perseus holds the head of Medusa

CHAPTER 7

THE STORIES OF HOMER

The rich civilization of the Mycenean warriors would have been completely forgotten were its memory not kept alive in the legends recited by generations of storytellers (called bards) who lived after the Dorian invasion. During the grim years of the Dark Ages, the Greeks loved to listen to tales of the military exploits of the Mycenean heroes. Townspeople would gather eagerly around a central hearth in the evening to hear an itinerant bard describe the dramatic events of the heroic age that preceded their own simpler times.

The legends were usually recited or chanted in verse to the accompaniment of a lyre, an ancient stringed instrument resembling a small harp. These story-poems are called epics (from the Greek *epos* meaning "tale"). Since many of them were too long to be entirely memorized (recitations could last for hours), the storyteller would simply remember the basic plot as well as key words and phrases, repeating some of them at

specific intervals. He would then improvise the verses in between as he went along. For this reason, each version of an epic was unique, although key phrases occurred again and again in all of them.

Homer

Around 750 B.C.E. a bard named Homer (born on the Aegean island of Chios) composed two long epics set in Mycenean times—*The Iliad* and *The Odyssey*. Similar stories had been told for hundreds of years, but Homer refined them and created the definitive versions which other bards subsequently recited, as accurately as they could, until the words were finally written down. Homer was the first to actually describe the physical appearance and personalities of the gods and goddesses, and his epics are filled with lively episodes in which the deities intercede in the lives of the human characters.

According to legend, Homer, history's first great poet, was blind. However, now that the alphabet was in use, other poets of his time copied down his epics. Some scholars believe that the need to record Homer's works was the crucial factor that inspired the Greeks to develop the written language. Homer's works soon became an important part of the Greek cultural heritage, and Peisistratus (the tyrant who ruled Athens after Solon) commissioned a group of writers to prepare a definitive text of *The Iliad* and *The Odyssey*.

These epics are considered the greatest poems in ancient Greek literature, and they

A bard

are still read and enjoyed today. They are of great historical value as well, for they provide us with a detailed record of life in Greece during the Bronze Age and the Archaic period.

The Iliad

The first of the two epics, *The Iliad*, describes the final days of the war between Mycenae and Troy (the Greeks called it *Ilium*). Homer's story, more fanciful than the historical account we read about in Chapter 3, attributes the cause of the Trojan War to the vanity of three Greek goddesses. The story begins when Paris, a young prince of Troy, is told to choose who among the goddesses is most beautiful. When he selects Aphrodite, the goddess of love and beauty, she rewards him with the love of the most beautiful woman in the world. Her name is Helen, but unfortunately she is already married—to Menelaus, king of Sparta.

Paris visits Sparta, and when Menelaus is conveniently called away to a funeral in Crete, the prince whisks Helen off to Troy. Upon his return, Menelaus learns of the kidnapping and resolves to get Helen back. He turns for support to his brother Agamemnon, the king of Mycenae, and in a short time Menelaus, Agamemnon, and several other Greek kings set sail for Troy with their soldiers in a thousand ships.

The city of Troy is ruled by King Priam, father of Paris. It is surrounded by a huge, impenetrable stone wall. The Greeks lay siege to the city, but they cannot get inside the wall for ten years. From time to time the Trojans send out their best warriors to engage in hand-to-hand combat with Greek opponents, but the city itself remains invulnerable.

The Iliad focuses upon the events that occur at the very end of the siege. Homer relates how in the tenth year of the war a terrible plague infects the Greek camp. A soothsayer (someone who interprets the will of the gods and predicts the future) advises Agamemnon to release a woman captive (of whom he has grown fond) in order to end the plague. He releases the woman and replaces her with a slave girl belonging to another Greek king named Achilles.

Achilles is the greatest warrior in the Greek army, and he is very temperamental. Upon hearing that Agamemnon has taken his slave girl, he retires to his tent, where he sulks and refuses to fight the Trojans. At

Homer holding his lyre

this moment Hector, the older brother of Paris and the greatest of the Trojan warriors, suddenly appears outside his city's gates, challenging Achilles to combat. But the brooding king refuses the challenge, and he sends his best friend Patroclos to fight in his stead. Although he struggles valiantly, Patroclus is no match for Hector, and he is ultimately slain by him. The terrible news of the death of his friend finally draws Achilles from his tent. He chases Hector three times around the walls of Troy, and when at last the two men face each other in combat, Achilles kills the Trojan prince. He then ties Hector's legs to his chariot and drags his body around the city walls in triumph. The epic ends rather abruptly after King Priam of Troy begs for the return of his son's body for proper burial and Achilles honors the request.

The Iliad is a rich resource of information about the weapons and military strategies of the Mycenean Age, and it reveals much about the character of the Greek warriors themselves. For them, personal honor and courage were the highest of the manly virtues. Indeed, Achilles' greatest wish is to achieve glory: to die nobly on the field of battle and to be remembered by future generations for his valor. His wish is later granted.

The Odyssey

The fall of Troy is described in Homer's second epic, *The Odyssey*, a lively and exciting adventure story. It begins when Odysseus, the king of the Greek island of Ithaca, devises a plan to end the long siege. Following his orders, the Greeks build a huge wooden horse, place it outside the Trojan city gates, and then pretend to sail home. The Trojans, believing the horse to be a peace offering, open their gates and drag it inside. Unknown to them, inside the belly of the horse are several armed Greek soldiers, led by Odysseus himself. There is, of course, much feasting and celebrating in Troy. That night, while the Trojans are slumbering, the Greeks climb out of the horse and open the gates of the city for their comrades (who have sailed back). The Greeks destroy the city, kill most of the Trojans, and free Helen. She returns to Menelaus (who forgives her for everything).

Much of *The Odyssey* describes the many obstacles that Odysseus encounters on his voyage home, a voyage that should have required only a few weeks but instead takes ten long years. He encounters many formidable adversaries, including Polyphemus, a one-eyed Cyclops; the man-eating giants, the Laestrygonians; the lovely enchantress Circe, who turns men into pigs; the Lotus-eaters, who give him a plant to eat that makes him forget about returning home; the bird-like Sirens, whose song no man can resist; and the many-headed monster, Scylla. Homer's colorful descriptions of the

Vintage engraving of the Trojan Horse

adventures of Odysseus and his men make this an action-packed story that is hard to put down. Nor do the king's troubles end with his arrival home, for he then has to deal with the persistent suitors of his faithful wife Penelope who have turned his palace into a hotbed of decadence. Luckily, Odysseus has Athena on his side, and that makes all the difference. (The goddess of wisdom admires his intelligence.)

Odysseus embodies the character traits the Greeks most respected: wit, cunning, and resourcefulness. He is also courageous and honorable. Against seemingly impossible odds, he outsmarts his opponents and regains his kingdom. And yet, Odysseus is not perfect, for he cannot resist the opportunity to boast of his achievements. This, in fact, is what causes his journey home to be so treacherous and drawn out. The Greeks considered excessive pride (*hubris*) among the worst of human weaknesses. The tale of Odysseus shows what can happen to someone who is too proud.

Ancient wall painting of the blinding of Polyphemus

Historical Accuracy

Although Homer's two great epics appear to describe life during the Mycenean age, it is important to remember that the poet lived hundreds of years after the fall of Troy. For this reason, many of his descriptions actually apply to his own times while others reflect his impression of what life *might* have been like in the earlier age. So *The Iliad* and *The Odyssey* provide a great wealth of information about both the Mycenean Age *and* the Archaic Age. The challenge to us is to decide which descriptions belong to which period.

Until fairly recently, scholars thought that Homer's stories concerned imaginary happenings in imaginary places. They considered the two epics outstanding pieces of literature, but no one thought that they might be based upon historical fact. In the

Polyphemus, the Cyclops.

next chapter, you'll find out how wrong they were.

Questions

1. How were the early epics recited?
2. What are the names of Homer's two great works?
3. According to Homer, what caused the Trojan War?
4. What was Achilles' greatest wish?
5. What does The Iliad tell us about the character of the Mycenean warriors?
6. What was Odysseus' clever plan to end the siege?
7. How long did it take Odysseus to return home?
8. Describe Odysseus' personality.
9. Are Homer's works historically accurate?

Further Thoughts

1. In *The Odyssey* Homer describes a beautiful island named Phaeacia where the people love dancing, hot baths, and comfortable beds. The men are skillful sailors and merchants. Scholars believe that Homer was thinking of Crete when he wrote about this island paradise.

2. The works of Homer were known in Africa as well as Europe. In the last century, over six hundred ancient papyrus texts were discovered in Egypt that contained parts of the famous Greek epics.

3. It took the ancient bards a long time to recite an epic. They usually covered one section each evening. To get an idea of how long an entire recitation took, consider the case of a sixty-year-old man who recently recited a poem the length of *The Odyssey*. Reading aloud for two hours in the morning and another two hours in the afternoon, he required two weeks to complete the work!

Projects

1. "Beware of Greeks bearing gifts" is an expression frequently used in modern everyday conversation. What is the derivation of this expression and what does it mean? Write a short paragraph that describes an example or two that illustrate the truth of this expression. (Marc Aronson, a student at Fay School, suggests that "Beware of gifts bearing Greeks" is an equally valid warning.)

2. Read as much as you can of a modern edition of *The Iliad* or *The Odyssey*. There are many versions available that were written for middle school students. Especially recommended are two books by Dorothy Sutcliffe: *Black Ships Before Troy* and *The Wanderings of Odysseus*. Also recommended is *The Odyssey* by Geraldine McCaughrean (Puffin Classics).

3. Iphigenia was the daughter of King Agamemnon. Her story is told in the short book *A Fair Wind for Troy* by Doris Gates. Read the book or find another resource about her and write a short report.

4. Achilles was the son of a nymph (Thetis) and a mortal man, so he was half-immortal. Today "Achilles' heel" refers to a vulnerable spot. Look up the story of Achilles and find out why his heel was vulnerable. How was his vulnerability used against him in the Trojan War?

5. Do you accept Achilles' ideal of living a short but glorious life rather than a long, uneventful one? Why, or why not? Write a paragraph explaining your point of view.

6. What is the meaning of the expression, "her face launched one thousand ships?"

7. Originally the word "odyssey" simply meant the story of Odysseus. What does it mean today? Honda makes a car called an Odyssey. Why is this a good name for a car? What other products might be given this name?

8. Cassandra tried to warn the Trojans about the wooden horse. Consult a book on mythology and find out why the Trojans did not accept her advice. At the same time, find out what finally happened to Paris. Do you think he met with an appropriate end? Write a short report about these two colorful Trojans.

Ancient statue of the dying Achilles

CHAPTER 8

IN SEARCH OF HOMER'S CITIES

Heinrich Schliemann was a German businessman who believed that the stories about Troy and Mycenae actually took place. As a child, he had listened with rapt attention as his father read to him passages from *The Iliad* and *The Odyssey*, and from an early age he determined to find the places described so vividly in Homer's works. Schliemann had little money but a great deal of ambition. His formal schooling was minimal, but he read every book he could get his hands upon and became a self-educated man. He even taught himself eighteen languages.

Schliemann realized that his projects would be very expensive. He knew he had a good business sense, and so he became a trade merchant, traveling to many parts of the world in search of products that he could sell profitably. By his mid-forties he had amassed a small fortune. Now he was able to devote the rest of his life to that which interested him most: the search for the sites described in Homer's epics.

A Scientific Method

He began his quest for Troy in 1870 at Hissarlik, a small Turkish town built above a broad plain and overlooking the Dardanelles. The local geography seemed to match Homer's description of the region surrounding the walled city of King Priam. Better yet, a huge mound of earth protruded above the level area of the town, and Schliemann suspected that it might contain artifacts dating from the ancient past.

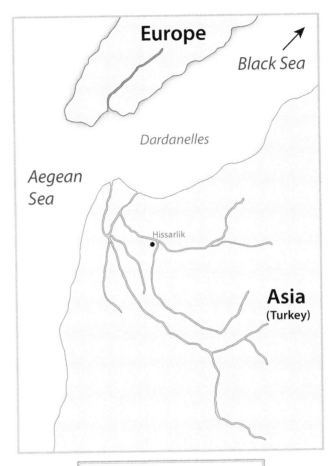

Site of Troy in western Turkey

Archaeologists call a mound of earth made up of the ruins of an early culture a *tel*.

Schliemann hired over one hundred workmen to help him excavate the *tel*. He approached the digging in a systematic way, organizing the site into many small sections. He carefully recorded his findings so that the original configuration of soils, rocks and buried materials could be studied at a later time. This was a novel approach, because up until then most people digging for ancient artifacts were basically treasure hunters. They shoveled aggressively in the soil, tossing aside any objects that were broken or made of inferior materials as they looked

The map labels: Europe, Black Sea, Dardanelles, Aegean Sea, Hissarlik, Asia (Turkey).

for priceless objects in "mint" condition. As a result, many fragments of ancient pottery, broken tools and weapons—priceless clues to the past—were lost or even destroyed. (This was before Sir Arthur Evans unearthed fragments of the Minoan civilization in Crete.)

Schliemann's interest was not to become rich (he already was) but rather to learn about long-gone civilizations. He established a method that, with many refinements, is followed by archaeologists to this day. For this reason, Schliemann is considered the Father of Scientific Excavation.

Multiple Troys

The *tel* at Hissarlik turned out to be the most complex archaeological site ever excavated until that time. As his workers cut through the layers of earth, Schliemann unearthed the remains of not one but nine cities that had been built one on top of the other.

The reason for the layering of cities is simple. Like most peoples of the ancient Mediterranean world, the Trojans had built their homes of mud-bricks. When the walls of a house became old and unstable, they were simply knocked down, and a new house was built upon the same site. In the case of fire, earthquake or general destruction caused by war, an entire city might be reduced to rubble and abandoned. What if another group of people happened along at a later time and decided they liked the site? They would simply level off the area and build their houses over the now-covered ruins of the earlier city. In the case of a strategically placed site like that of Troy, centuries of building one settlement or city upon the site

of an earlier one gradually resulted in the formation of a mound of earth made up of many layers. Each layer represented one city, the oldest lying at the bottom and the most recent at the top. For a modern archaeologist, digging into a large *tel* is something like slicing through a many-layered cake.

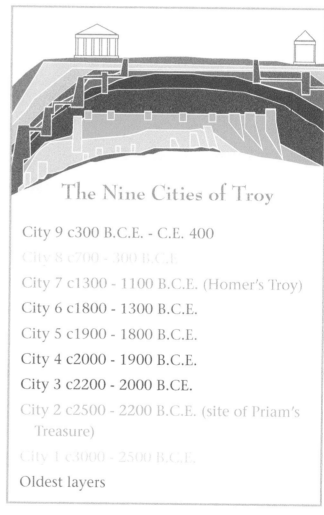

The Nine Cities of Troy

City 9 c300 B.C.E. - C.E. 400

City 8 c700 - 300 B.C.E.

City 7 c1300 - 1100 B.C.E. (Homer's Troy)

City 6 c1800 - 1300 B.C.E.

City 5 c1900 - 1800 B.C.E.

City 4 c2000 - 1900 B.C.E.

City 3 c2200 - 2000 B.CE.

City 2 c2500 - 2200 B.C.E. (site of Priam's Treasure)

City 1 c3000 - 2500 B.C.E.

Oldest layers

In the second layer (city 2) Schliemann uncovered the ruins of fine houses and strong fortifications. He found an altar that had been used for sacrifices, a paved road and even the remains of a palace. Surely, this was an important ancient city. When a workman chipping at the hardened sediment with his shovel suddenly struck something smooth and shiny, Schliemann was called to the spot. As he gently knocked away the pieces of rock, Schliemann realized that he was uncovering a cache of ancient artifacts. He was overjoyed, but he tried not to reveal his excitement. According to his written account, he told his workers to take off the rest of the day. They must have been delighted with the unexpected holiday, and their employer was now free to uncover the buried treasure in private. Once he was alone with his wife Sophie, he carefully uncovered a priceless collection of gold cups and vessels, silver vases, copper daggers, and gold jewelry. Over eight thousand priceless articles had lain buried in the earth for over three thousand years! He called these objects "King Priam's Treasure." (Priam, remember, was the King of Troy in *The Iliad*.) For Schliemann, they were proof that he had uncovered Homer's Troy.

Recently, however, archaeologists using sophisticated scientific technology have concluded that it was the seventh city, and not the second, that Homer described in *The Iliad*. The objects found by Schliemann were buried hundreds of years before the Trojan War took place. Actually, the fact that they belonged to an earlier period makes their discovery even more important than Schliemann believed it to be. They are the works of craftsmen who lived long before the Greeks built their stone citadels on the Peloponnese.

Although he was very methodical by the standards of his time, Schliemann did make some clumsy mistakes. For example, in an effort to create a cross section of the site, he dug a huge trench across a major part of the *tel*, shoveling away everything in his path. Fortunately, his detailed journal contains useful data about some of the materials that were shoveled from the trenches. But his

efforts to uncover the second city damaged a large portion of the ruins of buildings and walls that made up the more recent seventh city—Homer's Troy, the very city he had been seeking.

Schliemann had ordered his workers to take the rest of the day off because he wanted to keep his discoveries for himself. He felt no obligation to share "Priam's Treasure" with the Turkish government, and so he smuggled it to Germany. The Turks were furious when they found out what he had done, and they refused to let him dig in Hissarlik any longer. Schliemann offered to write a check to cover the artifacts he had taken, but this offer was not accepted.

So Schliemann left Turkey and sailed to Greece. The year was 1894. Why Greece? Think about the valiant warriors who battled the Trojans in *The Iliad* and of King Agamemnon who led them. Confident that he had found Homer's Troy, Schliemann was now eager to discover the remains of the ancient kingdom of Mycenae.

The Citadel at Mycenae

There was no mystery about the location of the site of the Mycenean citadel, since the ancient walls had remained visible since the days of the Dorians. Schliemann employed 150 workers to dig there for him.

The structure of the wall itself was of great interest to him. Built of huge limestone blocks that fit snugly together, it was twenty-three feet thick and (in some places) sixty feet high. At about the time of the destruction of Knossos, a Mycenean king had rebuilt the hilltop palace buildings and reinforced the wall. Its sheer massiveness indicates how concerned the early Greeks were about war and the defense of their cities. When the Dorians became a dangerous threat in the twelfth century B.C.E., the wall of Mycenae was extended around an underground spring in order to insure a supply of fresh water during a state of siege.

The entrance gate to the citadel was capped with a magnificent stone relief sculpture of two (now headless) lions on either side of a tall column. Originally the lions had faces of colored stone or gilded bronze that were pegged into holes in the background stone slab. Their eyes, probably made of glistening gems, would have looked down majestically upon those who entered the citadel. The lion gate is one of the earliest coats-of-arms in history—the lions signify the power of the king as he defends his city (represented by the column).

Mycenae had been excavated by others before Schliemann arrived upon the scene. A huge tomb built in the shape of a beehive

(called a tholos tomb) had been discovered outside the walls of the citadel. A tholos tomb was basically an earth-covered mound with a stone interior; a long entrance passage led to the conical chamber. The tomb's beehive shape was formed by rings of carefully cut stones, each ring slightly smaller than the one immediately below it. Tholos tombs had been built for the kings of Mycenae between 1500 and 1200 B.C.E. Similar structures that must have served as models for the Greeks have been found in Crete.

The chamber of the tholos tomb at Mycenae was huge, measuring nearly fifty feet in width and height. It had originally been filled with gold and bronze objects; the body had been buried in a pit within the chamber. Schliemann visited the tomb when he arrived at Mycenae. He called it the Treasury of Atreus, because since ancient times it had been believed that Atreus,

The lion gate

Interior of tholos tomb

knew the language of the classical Greeks, and he had read the diary of a Greek traveler named Pausanias who had visited Mycenae as a tourist 1,600 years earlier. Pausanias had observed stone gravestones marking the tombs of Agamemnon and some of his followers, and he noted in his diary that these were located within high stone walls. And so while many people scoffed at his decision to dig within the walls of the citadel, insisting that he was looking in the wrong place, Schliemann broke the ground just inside the main gate.

His efforts were amply rewarded. Not far below the surface he found a round double fence of stone slabs, known to modern archaeologists as Grave Circle A—the fence encircled five upright gravestones. Excitedly,

father of King Agamemnon, had been buried there. Although the contents had been plundered long ago, the structure of the tomb revealed the impressive architectural skill of the Mycenean builders. Furthermore, the vastness of the tomb suggested that the king who ordered it built possessed great wealth and power. Sadly enough, at the time Schliemann visited the tomb it was being used as a sheepfold.

Schliemann's appetite for a dramatic discovery in Mycenae had been whetted by his success in Hissarlik. He reasoned that if he could locate the major tombs of the other Mycenean kings, he might find golden objects as extraordinary as those in Priam's Treasure. Since the tholos tomb and a few smaller graves had been found outside the city walls, scholars assumed that any other tombs would lie in the same vicinity. Schliemann, however, had other ideas. He

Ruins of Mycennae

Schliemann dug beneath the gravestones and discovered five deep shafts that had been cut into the rock. These were the undisturbed tombs of a royal cemetery predating the graves found outside the walls. At the bottoms of the shafts lay nineteen skeletons, buried in rich garments lavishly decorated with gold. A small baby's skeleton was dressed in a complete suit of gold. Five of the men had beautiful golden death masks placed on their faces. They were the same type of mask that the ancient Egyptians placed upon the faces of their royal mummies.

Around the skeletons were scattered a vast number of valuable personal possessions such as gold bracelets, signets, diadems, drinking cups of gold and silver, vases, swords and daggers, mirrors, and golden breastplates. One of the cups so closely resembled the one belonging to King Nestor described in *The Odyssey* that Schliemann immediately referred to it as "Nestor's cup."

Nothing like this had ever been found before in Greece. Those artifacts that had been recovered at other sites were of very different styles and dated from later periods. Schliemann was ecstatic. Homer had mentioned that Mycenae was "rich in gold," and these objects seemed to prove that he was right! In fact, more gold was found in these shafts than in all the other Greek sites excavated up to the present time.

Just as he "knew" he had found Homer's Troy, Schliemann was convinced that he had found the tomb of the children of Atreus (Agamemnon and his siblings). As he lifted one of the golden masks to the light, he dramatically exclaimed, "I have looked upon the face of Agamemnon!" But once again he was mistaken, for the mask as well as the other articles in the graves had been buried four centuries before Agamemnon was born. Modern archaeologists, noting the Cretan influence in the elaborate handles of the daggers and in the lines of the cups and the jewelry, confirm that the graves date from early Minoan times.

The objects found in the Mycenean graves are of great historic value. Many of

The *"mask of Agamemnon"*

the golden cups and plates are decorated with scenes from daily life, and these are excellent records of the dress and activities of the early Myceneans. A bronze dagger is decorated with pictures of hunters carrying huge shields and battling lions. The graves also bear witness to the extensiveness of the Mycennean trade network, for they contain silver stags from Anatolia, ropes embossed with amber stones from the region of the Black Sea, and ostrich eggs from Nubia (the African kingdom south of Egypt).

Schliemann's inaccurate estimate of the dates of the Mycenean shaft graves does not lessen the importance of his discoveries. To the contrary, the ancient Greek culture probably changed very little during the few hundred years separating the craftsman who made the golden masks and the warriors who fought at Troy.

Discoveries by Later Archaeologists

Other tholos tombs have been discovered since Schliemann's time. Many of these were used for multiple burials, and one has been found that contains twenty skeletons. Apparently, when an important person died, the tomb was reopened and the old bones were simply moved out of the way to make room for the new ones! Given their massive size, these tombs must have been built for the kings and their families. Who else could have afforded such grand final resting places? Nine tholos tombs have been discovered in Mycenae, while forty have been located at the sites of other Bronze Age cities. Some of the tombs still contained valuable objects, including a suit of bronze body armor and several metal helmets decorated with boars' tusks that closely resemble those described in *The Iliad*.

Other smaller gravesites called dromos tombs have also been discovered; more crudely constructed than the tholos tombs, the dromos tombs are basically long, narrow caves. Several hundreds of these smaller burial sites have been excavated in and around Mycenae. They probably once held the bodies of high-ranking warriors and their families.

Since Schliemann's day, the remains of the buildings of the citadel have been carefully unearthed. They are grouped around a courtyard. The palace itself has a large hall (called a *megaron*) surrounded by wide stone pillars; in the center of the hall is a circular hearth. On the right, against the wall and facing the hearth, stands the king's throne. Similar megarons have been uncovered in other Mycenean citadels in Tiryns and Pylos. They strongly resemble the main room in Odysseus' palace described in *The Odyssey*.

The walls of the Mycenean palace were once covered with bright frescoes, a further

Vintage map of Mycenae

indication of Minoan influence. Among the paintings that have survived are scenes of battle and wild boar hunts. Some of the Greek warriors depicted are carrying shields shaped like figure eights similar to those Homer described in *The Iliad*. Figure eight shields were also painted upon the walls of the palace of Knossos at the time of the occupation of the island by the Myceneans.

Schliemann's Later Years

Schliemann visited many parts of Greece and excavated extensively at the ancient citadel of Tiryns. Once again, he was guided by the writings of Pausanius. Toward the end of his life he traveled to Crete, where he hoped to purchase land in the vicinity of Knossos to look for clues to a civilization that he suspected was even older than Mycenae. He was unable to purchase the land, and so he reluctantly abandoned the project. He later regretted that he had not been more persistent, for he came to believe that Crete was the original site of the Mycenean civilization. As we have learned, his thesis was inaccurate. Yet, he had come closer than any other scholar to discovering the Aegean civilization that had flourished long before the fall of Troy. Sir Arthur Evans would begin his excavations in Crete ten years after Schliemann's death.

We owe a great deal to Heinrich Schliemann. Before he made his dramatic discoveries at Troy and Mycenae, historians believed that Greek civilization began in about the sixth century B.C.E. We now know that the great achievements of the Greeks living in the fifth century B.C.E. had their roots in the cultures of the peoples who settled on the rocky peninsula nearly fifteen centuries earlier.

Schliemann's work also showed that Homer's descriptions of the early Greeks were fairly accurate. Of course, those ancient epics must be read with an understanding that they were written centuries after the fall of Mycenae.

Questions

1. Why was Heinrich Schliemann considered a "self-made man?"

2. Why is Schliemann considered the Father of Scientific Excavation?"

3. Why were there so many Troys?

4. Describe Priam's Treasure.

5. What is a tholos tomb?

6. What is the lion gate?

7. Tell the story of the discovery of the golden "mask of Agamemnon".

8. What is a megaron?

9. Why did Schliemann want to dig in Crete?

10. Why is Schliemann so important?

Further Thoughts

1. Large sedimentary rocks that have been sliced through by blasts of dynamite line the highways in many parts of our country. The lines on these rocks resemble the layers that Schliemann found in the mound in Hissarlik. Look for these rocks as you ride along a turnpike, and when you see one, imagine that each line represents an important stage in an ancient culture. (Actually, each line does represent a specific geological era.)

2. Sir Arthur Evans, who unearthed remains of the Minoan civilization was greatly influenced and inspired by Schliemann as he oversaw the archaeological digs in Crete. Evans was a contemporary of Schliemann, although quite a bit younger. These two men, Schliemann and Evans, were the major pioneers in the study of the Bronze Age in ancient Greece.

3. Although Heinrich Schliemann was a brilliant man, he was also a great romantic. As we have learned, he loved the works of Homer so much that he desperately wanted to believe that he had found objects dating from the times described by the famous bard. Toward the end of his life, he began to realize that he lacked sufficient evidence to prove the authenticity of Priam's Treasure and Agamemnon's mask, and some scholars were even questioning whether he had found Homer's Troy. Such miscalculations seldom occur today, because modern technology enables archaeologists to date ancient artifacts with great accuracy.

4. Schliemann was "mad" about ancient Greece. Before he began his excavation projects, he advertised in a newspaper for a Greek wife. At the age of forty-seven he

chose a bride of nineteen from among the photos sent him. Fortunately, the marriage turned out well: Sophie adored her husband and considered him the most brilliant of men. She bore him two children, whom he named Andromache (the name of the wife of Hector) and Agamemnon (this is no surprise!). When the children were baptized, Schliemann laid a copy of *The Iliad* on their heads and recited one hundred verses aloud! He even named his servant Pelops, and his house in Athens was called Bellerophon (another figure from Greek mythology).

5.   It is important to remember that the artifacts discovered by archaeologists tell us but part of the history of an ancient people. Only the rich owned golden jewelry and bronze weapons, and only they were buried in stone tombs. The ordinary people wore jewelry made of flowers and were buried in the soil; not much is left of them or their possessions!

6.   The Turks sued Schliemann for its share of the gold he had found at Hissarlik, but their efforts were unsuccessful. When Schliemann began his digs in Mycenae, the Greek Archaeological Society sent an agent to keep an eye on his activities. This had an effect. When Schliemann found the so-called mask of Agamemnon, he cabled the Greek king to tell him about it. The mask and all of the treasures he found remained in Greece. The mask and many of the other objects can be seen today in the National Archaeologocial Museum in Athens.

Projects

1.   Archaeologists are working in many regions of the United States. Find out if there is a historical archaeological site near you, and write a short report about it.

2.   Unlike most ancient royal burial sites, the grave shafts at Mycenae were not robbed. Can you explain this? (Think about how deeply the shafts were dug) Write a report that justifies your opinion.

3.   Sophie Schliemann was an interesting woman. Find out what you can about her and write a short report.

4.   Priam's Treasure was kept in Berlin for many years. In 1945 it mysteriously disappeared, and it has only recently been recovered. What do you think happened to it and why? (Hint: this was during World War II) Write a short paper presenting your explanation for what happened.

5.   Think about the cities of Troy the next time you have a slice of many-layered cake for dessert!

6.   King Pelops established a famous dynasty at Mycenae. His most well-known descendants included Atreus, Agamemnon, Iphigenia, Orestes and Electra. But his family was doomed to suffer terribly because he once cheated in a chariot race. Find out more about the circumstances of the race. Then write a short play about what happened.

THE OLYMPIC GAMES

The Greeks held many festivals to honor their gods and goddesses. In fact, there were over seventy festival days each year. The most famous celebration was held in honor of Zeus every four years in Olympia, a religious sanctuary dedicated to the king of gods in the northwestern Peloponnese. Olympia lay nestled in a valley at the junction of two rivers near the foot of a hill named for Cronus.

The festival at Olympia was not only religious in nature. It was also a time for socializing and merry-making, and the acrobats, food peddlers, and athletic competitions created the atmosphere of a modern country fair. As more attention was focused upon the sporting events, the festival came to be known as the Olympic Games. Actually, competitive sports had long been a tradition even in those early times. They are vividly described in both of Homer's epics.

The Olympic Games were first held in July, 776 B.C.E., and they took place regularly for over one thousand years. The four-year period between festivals was known as an Olympiad. The Olympiads were numbered consecutively, and this division of time served as a useful system for dating important historical events in Greece.

The Evolution of the Olympic Games

At first only one athletic event was held at Zeus's festival. This was a 186-yard sprint (called the *dromos*) in which swift young men demonstrated their physical fitness and endurance by dashing across a field and back

again. The purpose of the race was to pay homage to Zeus. The first winner was a cook named Coroebos from the nearby town of Elis.

For fifty years the *dromos* remained the only athletic event at the festival, but eventually other races were added. When the Spartans took an active interest in the competitions, the program was further expanded to include a wide variety of contests. Actually, "athlete" comes from the Greek word *athlos* which means "contest." Over the years, the Olympic Games evolved into a long series of athletic competitions that were interspaced with religious ceremonies and literary presentations. By the fifth century, the festival had expanded to five days.

The Olympic Games eventually became so popular that during the week in mid-summer when they were held all fighting between city-states throughout Greece came to a halt. A national truce allowed the athletes to travel safely to Olympia, participate in the events, and then return to their stations on the battlefield. This was known as the Sacred Truce.

Contestants had to be of Greek lineage, and they came from as far away as colonies in Sicily and Ionia. Women were not allowed to attend the games (the athletes competed in the nude), but male slaves were welcome to observe the events. Greek women later created their own games called the *Heraea* (in honor of Hera) which were held every five years. These included running events for girls of different ages.

The Stadium

The Olympic running races took place on a wide track known as the stadium. The term "stadium" comes from the Greek word *stade*, meaning "one length of the track." Over 20,000 spectators could watch the races from the grassy embankments surrounding the stadium.

The long stretch of track had starting and finish lines at the two ends. The runners fitted their toes into grooved marble slabs. These were history's first starting blocks, and they can still be seen today in the ruins of the stadium. A blast of a trumpet signaled the beginning of a race. The clay surface was covered with sand to give the runners traction. According to Greek legend, the track measured six hundred feet because this was the distance that the legendary super-hero Heracles could run with one lungful of air.

The Other Events

Among the most popular Olympic events were the throwing of the discus (a nine to twelve-pound circular plate of bronze resembling a modern frisbee), the hurling of the javelin (a long spear), wrestling matches (no holds barred!), and boxing (without padded gloves). There was also a

standing broad jump in which the athlete grasped metal weights in his hands for added momentum.

Greek warriors had to be in top physical condition to fight in battle, and the ideal of the athletic soldier was dramatically demonstrated in a twelve hundred-foot dash in which the runners wore helmets and carried heavy shields. They must have felt incredibly encumbered.

A very odd and violent event was called the *pancratium*. This was a wild, free-for-

A discus thrower

all fight in which a contestant could box, wrestle, spit, kick and do just about anything except bite or gouge out his opponent's eyes! *Pancratium* means "all powers," and the athletes were probably huge and burly strongmen resembling our modern wrestlers. Milo of Crotono became a national hero because he won the *pancratium* seven times. He claimed that he developed his great strength by carrying a calf for an hour every day until it was a full grown bull!

The fight continued until one man held up his hand in defeat. Occasionally, there was a fight to the death. Arrachion of Phigalia, the winner of two previous pancratium crowns, died in a stranglehold. However, his dead body was awarded the victor's crown.

Not all wrestling events were this dangerous. In upright wrestling, a competitor simply had to throw his opponent to the ground three times. In ground wrestling, the two men struggled until one of them was pinned. The wrestling events took place in an arena called the *palaistra*.

Chariot racing was later added to the games, and the crowd was encouraged to wage bets on their favorites. The horses raced on a special oval track called a hippodrome. A wooden post marked the turning point at each end of the track. The chariots were pulled by teams of either two or four horses (depending upon the event), and a race consisted of twelve laps around the two posts. To begin the race, the horses lined up in a starting gate. These races were extremely dangerous; collisions and upsets were frequent occurrences. In one race, out of forty starters only one chariot finished.

In other races at the hippodrome the horses were ridden bareback by jockeys. One unusual event required the jockey to dismount at a certain point and run the last stretch while leading his horse. Many of the best horses came from Macedonia, a kingdom to the north of Greece. Although the Greeks considered the Macedonians crude and uncivilized, they allowed them to attend the Olympic Games so that they could view their magnificent steeds. In 356 B.C.E. King Philip II of Macedonia entered a stallion in a race at Olympia and won. On the same day his son Alexander was born. Philip thought that his victory was a good omen for his son, as indeed it was. We shall learn more of Alexander in Chapter 16.

The Greeks believed that it was important to excel in many areas, to be "well-rounded" rather than to specialize in only one skill. This ideal was reflected in the *pentathlon*,

Ruins of stadium at Olympia

a grueling competition of five events. Pentathlon means "five contests," and these included a footrace (a two hundred-yard dash), a discus throw, a long jump, a javelin throw, and wrestling. Contestants were eliminated in each event, and the victor of the last contest was the overall winner—the "pentathlete." This was the highest honor attainable at the Olympic Games.

Between the athletic competitions poets read their works and orators recited speeches about every subject imaginable. There were also contests between trumpeters, heralds, and painters.

Good Sportsmanship

The rules of the games were very precise, and it was considered a matter of personal honor to strictly adhere to them. Before any events took place, the athletes (and their trainers) swore an oath at the altar of Zeus to abide by the regulations and to practice good sportsmanship. The judges, resplendent in their purple robes, swore that they would accept no bribes!

Anyone found guilty of breaking a rule was eliminated from competition and forced to pay a fine. This was, of course, a great humiliation. The fine money was used to erect copper statues of Zeus (called *Zanes*), the bases of which were engraved with the names of athletes found guilty of cheating. The statues lined the entrance to the stadium and served as a reminder to the contestants to remain honest.

Upon conclusion of the athletic competitions, a procession of the champions as well as the judges marched to the Temple of Zeus. There the victorious athletes received garlands of wild olive branches cut with a golden knife from the trees of the sacred olive grove that grew near the temple. Even the statue of Zeus was crowned with a wreath of olive branches to signify his victory over the Titans.

After the awards ceremonies, the winners and other contestants feasted on the meat of hundreds of animals that had been sacrificed to Zeus, washing down the delicious food with liberal amounts of wine.

Olympic champions were considered heroes in their native city-states. Upon his return home, a victor traditionally drove a chariot pulled by four white horses through a special opening made in the city wall. He then placed his olive wreath on the altar of the patron god of his city. Afterwards, a banquet was held in his honor. Many champions enjoyed free meals for life. A

A winner's wreath

Spartan victor won the right to stand by his king in battle—for a warrior, this was the ultimate honor.

Sculptors made statues of the winning athletes, and these were proudly displayed throughout their home cities. Poets (the most famous was Pindar of Thebes) wrote odes in tribute to the champions.

Other Games

Although the games at Olympia were the most prestigious athletic contests, the Greeks held many other important festivals that included sporting events. Those competitions that were open to all Greeks were known as panhellenic ("all-Greek") games.

The Pythian Games were held in honor of Apollo every four years in the middle of each Olympiad at Delphi. Winners received crowns of laurel leaves, since the laurel was sacred to Apollo. The Pythian Games were especially famous for their competitions of lyre and flute players as well as their contests for original musical compositions (remember, Apollo was the god of music). These more creative events alternated with the usual running, jumping, and throwing competitions.

Every two years athletic games were held at Nemea and Corinth. The Nemean victors wore wreaths of wild parsley or celery, while those at the Isthmian Games in Corinth (held in honor of Poseidon) won wreaths of pine needles.

Athens was the site of the Panathenaic games. Most participants in these events were from Attica, but other Greeks were welcome as well. A winner was given an *amphora* (clay jar) filled with olive oil; this was an appropriate award, since, as we have learned, clay pottery and olive oil were the chief products of Athens. The amphora was decorated with a painting of the particular event in which it was won. This is the source of our modern tradition of awarding large cups to the winners of sporting tournaments. Smaller local festivals offered a variety of other awards, including pottery jars filled with wine, armor, weapons, and even money.

The Revival of the Olympic Games

The Olympic Games were held every four years until 394 C.E. By that time Greece had been conquered by the Romans, and the emperor Theodosius I cancelled the Games because he considered them pagan festivals that offended Christian religious doctrines. The tracks and arenas of Olympia soon fell into ruins, and the natural crumbling and decay caused by the passing of time were made worse by two violent earthquakes. The excitement and the glory of the games were forgotten until 1875 when the ruins of Olympia were uncovered by archaeologists.

The discovery of the ancient site aroused great interest in the Olympic Games among scholars. They studied the odes of Pindar in a new light, and they closely examined the paintings of competing athletes on ancient Greek jars and vases. The idea of drawing together athletes from many areas to compete in a spirit of mutual support and good sportsmanship has a timeless appeal. Baron Pierre de Coubertin, a French nobleman, was so inspired by the ideals of the ancient games that he worked tirelessly to convince the nations of the world to create a modern series of athletic contests. Thanks to him, the Olympic Games were resumed in 1896.

The first site of the new games was Athens (in honor of the first Olympians), and for nearly a century international competitions were held every four years in different cities throughout the world. Today, the games are staggered, with the winter sports taking place one year and the summer sports taking place two years later. For this reason, an Olympiad is now two rather than four years long.

Many of the traditions of the ancient Olympics have survived. For example, just as in early times an athlete lit a fire at the altar of Zeus to mark the beginning of the festival, a modern runner carries a torch and ignites the fire that burns throughout the period the Games take place in the host city. And the Greek tradition of fair play continues to inspire the athletes of the modern world.

Questions

1. Where is Olympia?
2. Why did the first Olympic Games take place?
3. Describe the stadium at Olympia.
4. What was the pancratium?
5. Describe the racing events at the games.
6. What cultural events took place at the games?

Modern Olympic torch

7. What was the highest honor an Olympian athlete could win?
8. How were the victors honored in their cities?

9. What are some other games that took place in ancient Greece?
10. How do the modern Olympics maintain the old traditions of the early Greeks?

Further Thoughts

1. There is a famous story about Callipatira, the mother of an athlete in ancient Greece who was determined to see her son compete. Since women were not allowed in Olympia during the events, she disguised herself as a man! Unfortunately, she was found out as she enthusiastically cheered her son on, but the officials were lenient. They understood her great pride in her son's athletic accomplishments, and so she was not punished.

2. A huge forty-foot high ivory and gold statue of Zeus created by the Greek sculptor Phidias once dominated the temple at Olympia. Its great beauty made it one of the seven wonders of the ancient world. Unfortunately, it disappeared long ago and we only know of its existence and appearance through ancient writings.

Reconstructed statue of Zeus at Olympia

3. The events of the Olympic Games tell us a lot about the daily lives of the ancient Greeks. The great distances between the city-states required men to become strong runners in order to carry messages from one city to another. The many brooks and streams that flow down the hillsides encouraged the young men to jump a relatively long distance, or else land in the water! (Greek pastures were not surrounded by fences, so athletes did not consider high jumping.) Of course, the spear was an essential weapon of the Greek soldier, and once he lost it, he might resort to throwing stones before he engaged in hand-to-hand combat. The skills required of young Greeks are clearly reflected in the foot race, broad jump, javelin throw, discus throw, and wrestling (and boxing) matches included in the athletic games.

4. Winning at Olympia brought great glory to the polis of the victor. Solon once offered five hundred drachmas (a great amount in those days) to any Athenian who won an olive wreath. When runner Leonidas of Rhodes won three events in each of four successive games, earning a record number of twelve olive wreaths, the people of Rhodes declared him a god!

Projects

1. One of the events of the modern Olympic Games is the pentathlon. Find out what this is and present a short report to the class.

2. Organize some athletic events for your class based on the original Olympic Games. Contestants can use frisbees as discuses and carry garbage can lids in the hoplite race. Use your imagination to plan other events, but do not include boxing or the pancratium! Write an oath of sportsmanship to be recited by the contestants at the beginning of the "games," and make some wreaths from the branches of a bush (forsythia makes excellent wreaths) for the winners.

3. Do a research project on the Olympic Games of modern times, showing their similarities to and differences from the original games. Who are some of the famous champions?

4. Some historians say that the Olympic Games developed from funeral games held in memory of the Greek hero Pelops. Find out about the story of Pelops' chariot race (if you haven't already done so), and write a short report.

5. Explain the meaning and derivation of the modern expression "resting on one's laurels." Give three examples.

6. Since 2008, the Paralympic Games have been held immediately after the Olympic Games in the host city. Find out what these games are and write a short report about them. Include the names of several contestants who have particularly distinguished themselves.

PART THREE
THE GOLDEN AGE

CHAPTER 10

THE PERSIAN WARS

Until the fifth century B.C.E., the city-states of mainland Greece remained aggressively independent. The only major confederation was the Peloponnesian League headed by Sparta. It was not until all of Greece was threatened by a powerful foreign army that the city-states were forced to forget their petty squabbles and join together in defense of their homeland. This occurred

known as the Father of History. We will refer to his writings from time to time.

A Mighty Empire

Persia was an ancient Asian civilization founded by nomads on the high plateaus of present-day Iran. In the mid-sixth century B.C.E. a Persian king named Cyrus began

The Persian Empire c. 490 BC

when the armies of Persia invaded Greece.

We know a great deal about the period of the Persian Wars because the battles were described in great detail by the Greek historian Herodotus. He was the first person to attempt to write a thorough account of the important historical events of his time in a systematic way. For this reason, he is

to extend his territory by conquering the lands of neighboring peoples. When he vanquished a tribe called the Medes, who had dominated western Asia up until then, he established the Persian Empire. (It was Cyrus who defeated King Croesus of Lydia.)

By 520 B.C.E. Cyrus's domain was huge. It spanned three continents, stretching from the Indus Valley in India westward to the bleak deserts of Libya and across Anatolia (including Ionia, which Cyrus conquered in 547 B.C.E.) to Thrace on the northeastern border of Greece. The distance from east to west was an incredible 2,700 miles. Encompassing nearly a million square miles, it was the most extensive empire the world had ever seen. Nearly half of the world's population lived within its borders. Persia had a well-organized government and was protected by a vast professional army.

The Ionian Revolt

Darius I became Emperor of Persia early in the fifth century B.C.E. Like all Persian monarchs, he was called "the Great King, king of kings ... king of this great earth far and wide." He divided his empire into twenty provinces called satrapies, each ruled by a governor (the satrap). Over the years, many of the satraps became very powerful men. Darius built a vast network of roads to link the parts of his empire. The Royal Highway was a paved road that ran 1500 miles from Susa (near the Persian Gulf) to Sardis (near the Aegean Sea). This made it easy for merchants as well as soldiers to travel across major parts of the empire.

The peoples who had been conquered by the Persians were forced to pay Darius tribute (a kind of tax) and to serve in the Persian army. This subjugation was particularly unbearable for the freedom-loving Greeks living in Ionia. In 499 B.C.E. Aristagoras, the tyrant ruler of

Miletus, led the Ionians in a revolt against Darius. They refused to pay any more tribute or to serve in the Persian army.

Aristagoras appealed to their country-men in mainland Greece to help them. Athens and Eretria (a city-state near Athens on the island of Euboea) responded with aid. Athens sent twenty ships and Eretria contributed five. Together the Ionian and mainland Greeks attacked and sacked Sardis, the regional capital and base of the local Persian satrap. Darius swore to avenge this act, and five years later he attacked and set fire to Miletus. The Ionian rebellion collapsed.

Darius Seeks Vengeance

Darius was furious that the armies from Athens and Euboea had supported the Ionians, and he was determined to punish them. So he dispatched an army and a fleet to mainland Greece under the command of

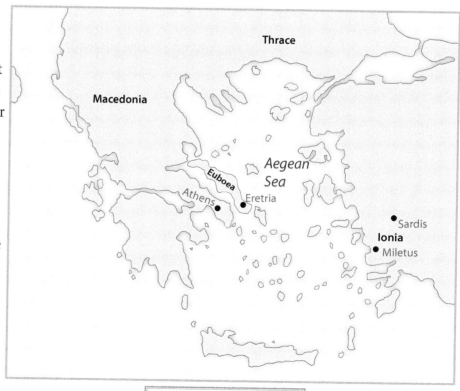

Ancient Greece and Ionia

his son-in-law, Mardonius. To their surprise, the Persians encountered violent resistance from the tribes of warriors living in Thrace and Macedonia (just north of Greece). Mardonius was wounded, and making matters worse, the Persian fleet was partially destroyed in a sudden storm. Darius' army had no choice but to return home.

In the spring of 492 B.C.E. Darius sent envoys to Greece to assess how much the Greeks opposed Persian authority. His men requested offerings of earth and water from the city-states they visited. This traditional gesture symbolized acceptance of a foreign government on land and sea. In many cases, the requests were granted. Athens and Sparta, however, felt differently. Herodotus tells us that the unfortunate envoy sent to Athens was unceremoniously thrown into a ditch and told to gather his own dirt. Similarly, the Spartans responded by heaving the Persian into a well, telling him to swallow as much water as he wished.

In 490 B.C.E. Darius summoned an army of some of his best warriors and sailed with them directly across the Aegean Sea to Greece. The Persians seized several Greek islands on the way. Darius' first goal was to destroy the port city of Eretria on the island of Euboea. From there he would move on south to deal with Athens. When his soldiers landed on Euboea, the local citizens staged a heroic resistance, but they were hopelessly outnumbered. Eretria was sacked. Temples and shrines were looted and burned, and the surviving Eretrians were enslaved.

A narrow strait separated Euboea from the mainland. As smoke filled the eastern sky, the Persians sailed across the calm waters and landed on the plain of Marathon. From there

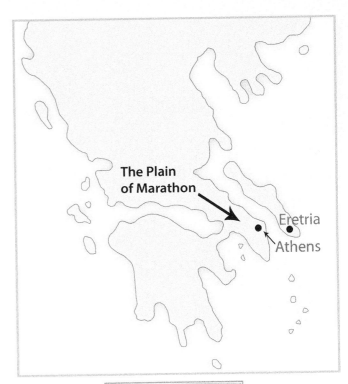

The area of Marathon

they planned to march to Athens, about 25 miles to the south.

The Athenian army raced northward to meet the invaders. The Greek soldiers must have trembled at the sight of the tall, fierce-looking Asian warriors who outnumbered them two to one. Miltiades, the Athenian general, had previously encountered Persian might while fighting in Thrace, and it was clear to him that the Athenians needed the help of the Spartan soldiers, the best fighters in all of Greece. A messenger named Pheidippides was recruited to run to Sparta for aid — according to legend, he covered the distance of 150 miles in only two days. But the timing couldn't have been worse. The Spartans were busy, partaking in a festival in honor of Apollo. They would send no soldiers to Marathon until their ceremonies ended at the next full moon. Pheidippides raced back to Marathon with the discouraging news.

A second runner was sent to Plataea, a city-state in Boeotia, with a similar request for aid. That city responded with a force of 600 men.

The Greek Advantages

Despite their fewer numbers, the Greeks did have some advantages as they faced the Persians. First of all, their foot soldiers were extremely well armed. Each man carried a six-foot spear (used for thrusting, not throwing) as well as a short sword. Furthermore, he was protected by bronze armor: a helmet adorned with a crest of dyed horsehair, a molded breast-plate, and greaves (which covered his lower leg). He carried a heavy round wooden shield called a *hoplon*, which explains why Greek foot soldiers were called *hoplites*. The *hoplon* was about three feet wide, bulging slightly outward toward the center but flat around the rim, where it was reinforced with a strip of bronze. A metal armband attached to the inner side enabled the *hoplite* to hold the shield steady.

Drawing of Greek Warrior on an ancient vase

The Persians were less well protected. They carried large wicker (wooden) shields covered with leather, and these could be easily pierced. They had no helmets (they wore cloth headdresses), nor did they wear body armor. And they carried spears that were somewhat shorter than those of the Greek hoplites.

A Persian Warrior

The greatest asset of the Greek army was its unique battle formation. Fighting strategies had changed drastically since the days of the Trojan War, when warrior heroes had ridden to battle in chariots and then dismounted to engage in hand-to-hand combat. Now the Greek *hoplites* marched shoulder to shoulder in a tight-knit configuration called a *phalanx*, one row of men directly behind another. The soldiers were protected by the solid line of their shields. As the *phalanx* marched forward, the spears of the first few ranks of soldiers were extended forward over the first rank of shields. Although the spear of a single soldier could be easily dealt with by an opponent, a long unbroken line of thrust spear points over a wall of shields was an intimidating sight.

Greek helmet

Armor breastplate

The Greek soldiers moved as a single unit, responding without hesitation to the orders of their commander. On the battlefield a *phalanx* would march steadily forward to the sound of a flute until it made physical contact with the opposing line of soldiers. As the men in the front ranks thrust their spears, they were pushed forward by the

weight of the rest of the hoplites marching behind them. So a battle was basically a shoving match, and the winner was the side that broke through the opposing line. Those men in the front ranks who fell were immediately replaced by those marching behind them. The *phalanx* was not a rigid formation. It could adopt different configurations, varying from a long thin line strung out across a wide field to a deep concentration only a few soldiers wide traversing a narrow mountain pass.

Since the soldiers carried their shields in their left hands, the right side of a *phalanx* was vulnerable, and one popular strategy was

Phalanx formation

to attack an enemy phalanx on that side. Sometimes wealthy Greek soldiers mounted on horses formed a cavalry that protected the vulnerable flanks of the phalanx. The Greek *phalanx* required constant training and strict discipline. It represented a team effort, and it was an incredibly effective offensive formation against any army that fought in the traditional free-for-all style of soldier against soldier.

Greek warriors

A final Greek advantage was a psychological one: The *hoplites* were fighting to defend their homeland against an invading enemy, and the sense of patriotism that filled their ranks fueled their determination to use every ounce of energy and strength against the foreign troops.

The major advantage of the Persians was, of course, their superior numbers. They also had a corps of archers much renowned for their skill.

The Battle Begins

Miltiades commanded an army of 10,000 Athenians and 1,000 Plateans against Persia's force of over 20,000. (Herodotus's descriptions of 100,000 Persians was greatly exaggerated.) His first move was to block the two exits from the Plain of Marathon. Then both sides waited. Perhaps the Athenians were hoping the Spartans would arrive. After five days, despite the overwhelming odds, Militiades attacked. He tried to compensate for his small numbers by thinly stretching his front line across the width of the plain and reducing the depth of the *phalanx* from eight ranks of men to four.

At the signal from their general, the Greek soldiers shouted their war cry to muster their courage and then charged. They crossed the plain at a run, making difficult targets for the enemy archers who were accustomed to slower moving opponents. The Persians must have been startled by the forceful assault, but they fought hard and aggressively.

The Persian center stood its ground. However, Miltiades had placed his best troops on the two flanks, and these soldiers

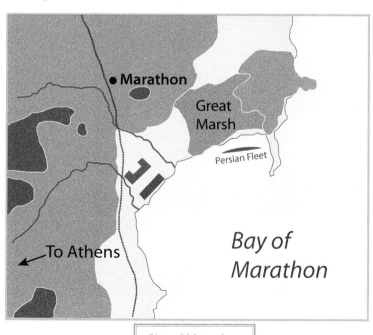

Marathon

Great Marsh

Persian Fleet

To Athens

Bay of Marathon

Site of Marathon

fought with such courage and force that they routed the opposing enemy wings. The Greek flanks then wheeled around to attack the enemy center from behind. The stunned Persian soldiers found themselves surrounded by gleaming Greek spears and swords. The Athenians fought on with a ferocity that would have impressed even the Spartans. In a short time, they were masters of the

scene of the Athenian victory. They were impressed.

The Greek dead were later buried in a common grave. The mound can still be seen today. Veterans of the battle were highly honored in their city-states for the rest of their lives.

According to legend, Miltiades sent a

Greek Double Envlopment at the Battle of Marathon

Greeks
Persians

field. Many of the retreating Persian soldiers got bogged down in a salt marsh that lay between the field of battle and the beach. A large number of them drowned, while others raced frantically toward their waiting ships.

No one could have predicted the Greek victory at Marathon, and Miltiades must have been ecstatic. In a triumph of cunning and teamwork over brute strength, he had lost only 203 men to the Persians' 6,400. When the Spartans later arrived at the battlefield, they gazed silently upon the

runner, the same Pheidippides who had raced to Sparta, to carry news of the victory to Athens. Exhausted by all the running he had done as well as the day's battle, the gallant messenger had only enough strength left as he staggered through the city's gate to gasp, "Niki!" (Victory!). Then he fell down—dead. Although Pheidippides was only a legendary figure, he has come to embody the courage and endurance of the ancient Greek army.

The twenty odd miles he had run from Marathon to Athens has become the model for modern footraces, called marathons, over a similar distance. When the Olympic Games were revived, the marathon became one of the events. The first Olympic marathon was won by Spiridon Louis, a Greek postal worker, with a time of 2 hours, 58 minutes.

Meanwhile, the Greek army proceeded to the outskirts of Athens to take up defensive positions. The Persian fleet was undoubtedly unsettled by the array of soldiers lining the shore. The enemy ships hastily picked up their straggling troops and withdrew to Asia.

The Athenians were overjoyed. They had proven that their determined *hoplites* could stand up against as mighty a foe as the Persian army. But they worried that they had not seen the last of their enemy. As it turned out, they had simply won breathing time. The Persian invasion made it clear to the Greeks that they had to take precautions against future attacks. To strengthen security, thirty-one city-states formed an alliance, promising to aid each other if they were threatened by outside forces. This new *Panhellenic* ("all Greek") League was led by Athens and Sparta.

After the death of Miltiades, the Athenian forces were placed under the command of a wise politician named Themistocles. He believed that the city needed a strong navy to defend itself. The timely discovery of veins of silver in the hills of Attica helped Athens to finance the building of a fleet of two hundred ships.

The Persians Return

Darius died soon after his crushing defeat at Marathon, but his son Xerxes never forgot his father's humiliating loss, and he vowed to avenge it. In 480 B.C.E., ten years after Marathon, Xerxes invaded Europe with a huge army of 180,000 soldiers. Herodotus estimated the figure at over two million, but scholars agree that, once again, the historian exaggerated. Nonetheless, this was the largest armed force ever assembled. The troops came from many parts of the Persian Empire—among them were Babylonians, Armenians, Lydians, Syrians, Egyptians, Libyans, and Cypriots. The soldiers seemed a motley crew with their differing styles of dress and types of weapons, and they spoke a wide variety of languages.

Xerxes moved his vast army across the 3/4 mile wide expanse of waters of the Hellespont by lashing together over 600 boats to build a double pontoon bridge. Two rows of boats were lined up side-by-side. They were held in place by great boulders of rock that had been tied to long ropes and thrown into the sea bed (primitive but effective anchors). Other ropes joined the ships together. Wooden planks were then placed across the hulls of the ships and laid across the ropes that held the vessels together. They formed a long wooden bridge

A bridge of ships

stretching across the ships from shore to shore. The planks were covered with dirt and straw to fill in the gaps between them, and canvas sails were layered over the side railings. These measures prevented the horses and cattle that were led across the bridge from seeing the sea and stampeding. It took seven days and seven nights for Xerxes' entire army to march across the bridge.

When they were safely ashore on European soil, the Persian army began making its way across Thrace toward Thessaly. The soldiers were supplied by the fleet of ships that followed them along the coast, although rumors circulated in Greece that the enemy troops were drinking the rivers dry. To avoid the dangerous waters at the cape of Mount Athos (Mardonius had lost many ships there ten years earlier), Xerxes ordered that a canal be dug across the isthmus. This was a distance of a mile and a quarter. Traces of the canal are still visible today.

Meanwhile, the Athenians were busily preparing for the worst. They consulted the Oracle of Delphi, asking the Pythia how they could best defend their city against the Persians. To their horror, the oracle predicted disaster and advised the Athenians to flee for their lives! The only hope, she added, lay in "the wooden walls." As usual, the oracle's message was vague and offered multiple interpretations. What were the wooden walls? Some men thought of the wooden palisade that surrounded the Acropolis, and they concluded that the city's population should seek shelter behind them. Themistocles, however, was convinced that the wooden walls were the sides of his newly built fleet of ships. He believed that the

Xerxes marches to Greece

Athenians' only hope for survival against the Persians lay with their navy.

The Battle of Thermopylae

As the enemy troops moved closer to Greece, the Athenians and the Spartans formed a coalition: Athens agreed to send her fleet against the enemy warships, while the Spartans were to take command on the fields of battle. Everyone agreed that this was an excellent division of resources.

The Greeks decided to make a stand against the Persians at the Pass of Thermopylae ("the gate by the hot springs") on the southern border of Thessaly. This narrow piece of beach between a sheer mountain wall and the sea was the major route from north to south. The Spartans knew that their numbers were greatly inferior to those of the vast Persian army, and they hoped to lessen their disadvantage by bunching their men as tightly as possible in

The beach at Thermopylae

the 50-foot-wide pass. Since only a limited number of enemy soldiers could crowd onto the beach at one time, the Greek hoplites had a reasonable chance of holding their line against the invaders.

The Greek army that assembled at Thermopylae was led by Leonidas, king of Sparta. His 8,000 soldiers included 300 members of the Spartan royal bodyguard. He posted 1,000 men at the southern entry to the pass to protect the rear of his army. When one of the Spartans heard a Persian envoy warn that the arrows of the enemy archers would darken the sky, he confidently replied, "So much the better. We can fight in the shade!"

Themistocles commanded the fleet that was moored just north of the island of Euboea near Artemisium. The plan was for the Athenian ships to engage in frequent skirmishes on the high seas in an effort to prevent the Persian vessels from supplying their troops with food and weapons.

Xerxes' army waited near the pass for four days. Perhaps the generals were sizing up the Greek forces and planning their strategies. On the fifth day the Persians attacked. Leonidas and his men were ready. Manning an ancient wall, they ably repulsed every attempted assault. When the same

thing happened the next day, Xerxes must have wondered how he could turn things around to his own advantage. It was at this opportune moment that a Greek traitor named Ephialtes informed Xerxes of a mountain path leading to the other side of the pass behind the Spartans—just where Leonidas had placed his rear guard. That night, the heartless scoundrel (undoubtedly he was promised a large reward) personally led a contingent of Persians over the mountain; a full moon made it easy for them to follow the path. The sleeping Greek guard was caught by surprise and easily routed.

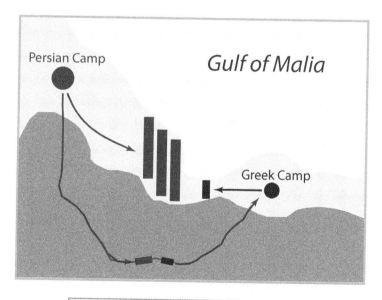

The Persians take the mountain pass

When Leonidas learned of the defeat of his rear guard, he hastily sent away most of his soldiers. He realized that he was trapped and that his cause was hopeless, but at least he could give his retreating men a chance to reach the safety of their comrades further south. According to legend, he told his remaining warriors to have a good breakfast, for later "we shall dine in (the kingdom of) Hades!"

Heroically, he led his own Spartan troops against what must have seemed like an infinite number of Persian soldiers. Herodotus describes how valiantly the Greeks fought, using their fists when their weapons were gone. In the end, their dead bodies were heaped upon each other at the entrance to the pass. Only two survived—one would be killed at a subsequent battle against the Persians, and the other killed himself on the spot at Thermopylae. For him the humiliation of defeat was too great to bear. Yet, the Spartans had held off the enemy long enough to insure the safe withdrawal of the rest of the Greek soldiers.

Although the Persians won the pass at Thermopylae, the reports of the courage of Leonidas and his men inspired the rest of the Greek army to pick up their fallen standard. To this day Leonidas is remembered as one of history's most gallant military leaders. A bronze statue of the Spartan king now guards the narrow pass. Nearby, a stone marker bears this moving epitaph to him and his three hundred warriors: "Go, stranger, and tell them in Sparta that we lie here in obedience to their orders."

The Destruction of Athens

When Themistocles heard of the massacre at Thermopylae, he immediately took the fleet south. The Persians, buoyed by their victory, marched triumphantly through the pass and then set up headquarters near Thebes. When they stormed the city of Athens, they found it nearly deserted. Most Athenians had fled and sought refuge on the island of Salamis and in Troezen (a city in the eastern Peloponnese). The Persian soldiers were greeted by the howling of abandoned dogs. Some of the pets did manage to escape, however. One account describes how a dog belonging to the family of the statesman Pericles (we'll learn more about him later) followed the retreating Athenians and even swam across the strait of Salamis, only to collapse and die from exhaustion on the island beach.

The Persians savagely killed the handful of men who had chosen to remain to

The statue of Leonidas at Thermopolae

defend their city, burned the temples on the Acropolis and plundered the shops and houses. They even burned Athena's sacred olive tree. (When the tree later sent out new green shoots, it became a symbol of the resilience of the Greek people.) The Athenians who had fled watched helplessly as the smoke from their burning city filled the evening sky.

The Battle of Salamis

The strait of water separating Salamis from the mainland of Greece is narrow and treacherous. As the Greek fleet waited nearby for the inevitable attack by the Persians, the wily Themistocles thought of a scheme to gain the upper hand. He sent a soldier to Xerxes under the guise of a traitor. The man was instructed to tell the Persian king that the Greek sailors were terrified of the enemy forces and were on the verge of retreat. Xerxes snatched the bait, and he immediately ordered his ships to sail to Salamis and attack the Greeks. He expected an easy victory.

The Greek ships were called triremes because they had three (*tri* means three in Greek) banks of fourteen-foot oars. One hundred and seventy rowers stroked the huge oars and kept in time by listening to the rhythmical sounds of a flute. A metal-ended battering ram extended below the waterline in the prow of each ship. In battle, a ship was rowed at top speed toward the side of an enemy vessel. As the battering ram crashed through the hull, it created a huge hole that caused the hold to fill with water. The hapless rowers of a sinking ship were then speared by

A trireme

the soldiers on the deck of the attacking vessel. Effective ramming depended upon the captain's mastery of force and speed—if the ship went too fast the ram would wedge too deeply and become stuck, while a slow approach would enable the enemy to get away. After ramming, a ship had to back up quickly so that the enemy sailors couldn't board its decks. An alternative strategy was to race parallel to an enemy vessel; just before pulling along side, the captain would order his oarsmen to pull in their oars. The attacking ship would then crash through the oars of the enemy vessel, breaking them as

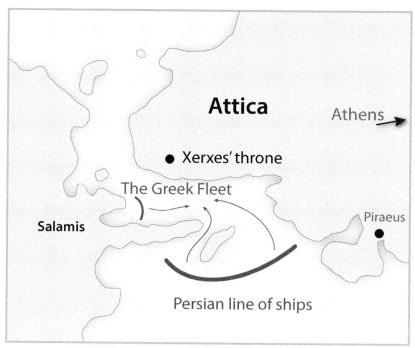

Attica

Athens

Xerxes' throne

The Greek Fleet

Salamis

Piraeus

Persian line of ships

The battle of Salamis

though they were matchsticks. Like Leonidas, Themistocles seized the advantage in spite of the smaller numbers of his forces by fighting in a confined area. The Greek sailors knew the channels and hidden reefs of their own waters better than an invading enemy possibly could, and their ships were nimbler. They couldn't expect to win a battle against the huge Persian fleet on the open seas, but the narrow strait of Salamis was a different matter.

When the Persian ships arrived at the strait, they quickly formed a solid line and moved slowly and deliberately toward the narrow row of Greek triremes guarding the entrance. The Greeks ships were outnumbered three to one. Xerxes, fully confident of a victory, had his golden throne set upon a hillside overlooking the strait. From there he planned to enjoy observing the destruction of the Greek navy.

Slowly, Themistocles' ships began to back water, the rowers softly chanting a hymn to Apollo. The Persians were delighted to see the Greeks withdrawing into the strait. They assumed that, as the "traitor" had predicted, the pathetic Greek captains were faltering in courage and attempting a slow and cowardly retreat. Responding to the shouts of their leaders, the Persian oarsmen rowed energetically, rapidly advancing toward the center of the continuously retreating Greek line. Soon the entire Persian fleet had been lured into the narrow strait. Themistocles now had the upper hand.

As the blare of a trumpet cut through the air, the Greeks attacked, crashing into the enemy vessels closest to the shores and driving the bewildered Persians into the center of the strait. Total confusion raged among Xerxes' captains as their ships smashed against each other. The Athenian seamen, anxious to avenge their still smoldering city, furiously rammed their triremes against the sides of the trapped vessels, breaking their oars, flooding their galleys, and driving them onto the rocks that lined the channel. Ship-wrecked Persian seamen were stabbed like fish by the triumphant Greeks!

The End of the War

Xerxes watched in horror as half of his ships were destroyed. Those Persian vessels that survived the onslaught quickly withdrew, signaling a total victory for the Greeks. The "Great King" led the bulk of his army back to the Hellespont and across the bridges to Asia. Persian messengers sailed across the Aegean and sped along the Royal Road from Sardis to Susa, bearing the news of the fiasco. Herodotus described how "neither snow, nor rain, nor heat, nor gloom of night stayed these couriers from the swift completion of their appointed rounds." If these words sound familiar, it is because they have become the unofficial motto of the U.S. Post Office.

Xerxes left behind a part of his army (about 70,000 men) under the command of his brother-in-law Mardonius. They were ordered to winter in Thessaly and to resume the attack the following year. (In those days, wars only took place during the good weather.) Meanwhile, the Greeks reveled in their victory.

The following summer (479 B.C.E.), a Spartan king named Pausanias led an army against the Persian troops at the plain of Plataea on Boeotia's southern border. (Pausanias was the regent for Leonidas' son.)

As usual, the Greeks were outnumbered, but the Spartans led them to victory. Mardonius was killed, as were most of his foot soldiers. Pausanias thus avenged Leonidas' defeat at Thermopylae, and once and for all the hated Persians were driven out of Greece. Herodotus noted with uncharacteristic understatement that the Persians "departed with altered minds" about the abilities of the Greek army and navy.

The same day as the battle of Platea, Greek triremes attacked and burned the Persian fleet while it was beached at Mycale on the coast of Anatolia. Afterwards, they moved on to free the Aegean islands and the Ionian cities from Persian rule.

The Persian Wars had come to an end, and the Spartan army and Athenian fleet were acknowledged as invincible forces throughout the Mediterranean world. In a surging spirit of patriotism, all the Greeks rejoiced at what they had accomplished. Had they not driven the world's mightiest army from their native soil? Throughout Greece every citizen was filled with pride and confidence, and the future looked bright indeed.

Questions

1. Who was Herodotus?
2. Why did the Ionian city-states revolt?
3. Why did Darius invade Greece?
4. What advantages did the Greek soldiers have over the Persians?
5. Describe the first marathon.
6. What was the prediction of the Oracle of Delphi regarding the Persian invasion?
7. Why did the Greeks lose at Thermopylae?
8. Describe a trireme.
9. How did Themistocles lure the Persian ships into the narrow strait?
10. Who finally drove the Persians out of Greece?

Further Thoughts

1. The distance between Marathon and Athens is a little over twenty miles. In the first modern Olympic Games, held in Greece, the marathon race was 24.8 miles (the distance from the Marathon Bridge to the Olympic stadium in Athens.) In the 1908 Olympic Games in London, the distance was changed to twenty-six miles so that the course would go by Windsor Palace. (They

even added 2.2 miles so the race would finish in front of the royal family's viewing box.) It has remained a race of twenty-six miles ever since.

2. When the Persians first arrived at Thermopylae, Xerxes sent a spy around the mountains to observe the Greek camp. He came back with the report that the Spartans were doing exercises and combing their long hair. At first the Persian king laughed at the image of such seemingly effeminate behavior, but his mood changed when one of his men informed him that the Spartans were the most valiant warriors in the land and that they always ceremoniously combed their long hair before fighting to the death.

3. From the start, the Greeks had little respect for the Persian culture. The Athenians in particular considered the Persian people little more than slaves ordered about by a tyrannical ruler. Didn't the Persian subjects approach their king on their knees? The Greeks didn't even kneel for their gods. The evolving Greek ideas about self-government and the worth of each individual contrasted dramatically with the Persians' unquestioning submission to their king. While the Greeks were bound together by a common language, religion and set of customs, apparently the Persian Empire could only be kept in line by the iron hand of a powerful monarch. When Darius invaded Greece, the defense of a new concept

of government was at stake. If the Persians had won the war, the Greek experiment in democracy would very likely have been snuffed out.

4. The average Greek hoplite carried nearly seventy pounds of equipment into battle. Remember that he had a heavy wooden shield and a long spear in addition to his armor and smaller weapons. It was thus crucial for him to spend a part of each day doing exercises that would build up his stamina. No wonder a strong body was considered one of the hallmarks of the ideal Greek man.

5. Xerxes' engineers had to construct two different sets of pontoon bridges. The first set was smashed by a violent storm that blew across the Mediterranean. Xerxes was furious, and he ordered the Hellespont punished. The waves were given three hundred lashes with a whip, branded with hot irons, and fettered (a pair of shackles was thrown into the water). The unfortunate engineers who built the bridges were beheaded.

6. The Immortals were an elite corps of the Persian army. Ten thousand of the best soldiers were hand-picked to serve in the corps. When one man was injured or killed, he was immediately replaced. This explains how they got their name. Xerxes' special bodyguard numbered one thousand

Immortals; each had a golden apple attached to the end of his spear. The other 9,000 had silver apples on their spears.

and Spartan fighters have returned to their native soil. Be imaginative, and back up your statements with solid reasons.

Projects

1. On a large piece of poster board draw a trireme. This can be an outer view or a cross-section. Consult books in the classroom or library for a good picture to copy. Label all the important parts of the ship.

2. Learn more about the Persian army. Make a chart, comparing and contrasting the weapons and fighting techniques of the Greeks and the Persians.

3. The first great historical account of a war was Herodotus' description of the Persian Wars. He was extremely interested in the causes of the east-west (Europe vs. Asia) conflict. Titled *The History*, a copy of this work is available in most large libraries as well as online. Find a copy and select some passages to read to the class.

4. Cyrus I was one of Persia's greatest monarchs. Find out about him and write a short report.

5. Croesus, King of Lydia, conquered Ionia, only to be conquered by Cyrus I. of Persia. We have already read about his predicaments (see Chapter 6). Find out more about this fascinating man, and write a short report.

6. At the conclusion of the Persian Wars, Athens and Sparta were the two "superpowers" of Greece. Yet, the governments and basic attitudes of the two city-states could not have been more opposite. Before reading any further, write a short essay describing what you think will probably happen next, once the Athenian

CHAPTER 11

ATHENS ACHIEVES GREATNESS

Although the Persians had been defeated, the Greeks could not be certain that they would not attack again in the future. The unified front presented by the city-states during the Persian Wars had been key to their victory against the invaders, and many Greeks believed that it was important to form a permanent alliance.

The Delian League

The Athenians led a movement to organize a group of city-states into a confederation. The cities located on the Aegean islands and in Ionia were quick to join, because they feared that they were easy prey for Persian warships. Eventually, there would be over 200 members. Each city in the confederation was asked to contribute either ships or a sum of money to build up a fleet that would patrol the extensive Greek coastline and protect its citizens from an enemy assault. Athens immediately offered her entire fleet of two hundred triremes.

The money collected was kept on Delos, an Aegean island sacred to Apollo (it was supposedly his birth-place), and for this reason the organization became known as the Delian League. It was led by Athens. To seal the alliance, the members dramatically hurled iron weights into the sea—this act symbolized their determination to support each other "until the iron floated to the surface." The Spartans had no interest in joining the League and remained the dominant power in the Peloponnese. We will learn more about them in the next chapter.

The Delian League functioned effectively for a while. The fleet grew large, and the isolated city-states of the Aegean were well protected. After twelve years the Greeks no longer feared the Persians, but when two member city-states (on the islands of Euboea and Samos) tried to withdraw from the

Athena, patron goddess of Athens

League, they were attacked by the Athenian fleet and bullied into submission. This made many of the other members uncomfortable. The Athenians exerted their authority in other ways as well. They claimed final jurisdiction over all court cases held in the League, and they demanded that all member cities use Athenian coins as well as the

Athenian system of weights and measures. They also ordered every city in the League to adopt a democratic government based upon the Athenian model.

In 454 B.C.E. the treasury was moved from Delos to Athens (supposedly for safeguarding). Before long, some of the money was being diverted for the rebuilding of major parts of that city (remember how it had been destroyed by the Persians?). This unauthorized use of funds caused bitter resentment among the League members, who had already begun to feel stifled by Athens. What had happened to the centuries-long tradition of independence and self-government? To many Greeks, it seemed that the Delian League had turned into the Athenian Empire.

But despite the grumbling, most of Greece was enjoying the benefits of peace and prosperity. Freed from the fear of foreign invasion, the people were able to devote their time and energy to practical pursuits. The Greek fleet eliminated the danger of pirates, and trade between mainland Greece and the rest of the Mediterranean world continued to expand.

The fifth century B.C.E. was to be the high point in the development of politics, imaginative writing, and art in ancient Greece. This blossoming of culture was centered in Athens. It is known as the Golden Age, or the Classical period of Greek civilization, and it lasted for about 200 years.

Democracy

As we have seen, the seeds of democracy were sown in very early times, and a way of life that respected individual liberties evolved in Athens during the centuries following the Dorian invasion. By 500 B.C.E. the Athenian government was neatly organized into three distinct branches. One, the legislative branch, dealt with the making of laws. This was the Ecclesia. Another, the judicial branch, was responsible for the interpretation of those laws when conflicts arose among the citizens. This branch was made up of a system of juries. The third, the executive branch, focused upon the enforcement of the laws. It consisted of the leaders of the government. Many of the other Greek city-states adopted a democratic form of government, but the system worked most effectively in Athens.

During the Golden Age the Ecclesia (the general assembly of citizens) met on a hillside just below the Acropolis called the Pnyx about once every ten days. All male citizens were expected to attend some of these sessions, but remember that only free adult male Greeks who owned land were

An owl was the companion and symbol of Athena

citizens—out of a population of 150,000, only about 40,000 met these qualifications.

At least 6,000 citizens had to be present for a meeting of the Ecclesia to take place. Sometimes, when there were no major issues to discuss, a smaller number of men showed up at the Pnyx. On these occasions, a quorum of citizens (the minimum number necessary to start the meeting) was herded up by special government officials using ropes dyed with wet red paint. If a citizen managed to slip out from the rope but picked up the tell-tale red stain on his clothing, he would be fined for non-attendance.

Every meeting opened with a prayer followed by the sacrifice of a pig to the gods. Then the discussion of public matters began. Any Athenian citizen could propose a new law or speak for (or against) someone else's proposal. Although only a fraction of the citizens attended a given meeting, and the citizens represented only a fraction of the total population of Athens, the Ecclesia was the closest thing to true democracy the world had ever known.

Every year, five hundred citizens were chosen by lot (at random) among the membership of the Ecclesia. These men made up the Boule, a council of 500. They handled the day-to-day running of the city. They also drew up a list of matters to be discussed by the Ecclesia, such as building and road repairs, the payment of city workers, and whether or not the city should go to war. Since no one could be on the Boule more than twice, the positions were passed around to a large number of men. Eventually, almost every Athenian citizen who regularly attended the Ecclesia meetings had a chance to serve on the Boule.

Whenever a crime was committed, a jury was chosen (again by lot) among the members of the Ecclesia. There were no judges, nor were there lawyers to represent clients. The accused person addressed the jury and pleaded his case himself (although a timid man was free to have a friend speak on his behalf). The Greeks considered public speaking an important skill, and at times like this a persuasive argument could determine the future of a man's life. The accused was allowed only six minutes to plead his case; the time was measured by *clepsydra* ("water-stealers"), a pair of clay pots set so that water dripped from one to the other in exactly six minutes. Then the jury (which could number from 101 to 1001 men) voted to determine the defendant's guilt or innocence.

Every juror was given two wheel-shaped bronze tokens. The token with a solid center was used to indicate innocence, while one with a hollow center represented guilt. At the end of a trial, the juror selected one of the two tokens and dropped it into a clay jar. Then the "votes" were counted. Should the accused be found guilty, the jury voted on the appropriate punishment.

An elite group of men known as the Ten Generals (the *Strategoi*) headed the executive branch of the Athenian government. They were elected annually by the Ecclesia and could serve an unlimited number of terms. They selected among themselves a Commander-in-chief who became the highest government official (like a president). The Ten Generals met every day and carried out the policies decided upon by the Boule and the Ecclesia. They also met with foreign envoys, discussed economic issues, supervised government officials such as tax collectors, and, if necessary, declared war. Occasionally, the Commander-in-chief delivered a speech to the public.

Ostracism

Years earlier, the archon Cleisthenes had devised an ingenious way to deal with those government leaders who seemed a threat to democracy. The Greeks loved order and harmony. The words "nothing in excess" that had been carved on the walls of the temple at Delphi reflected their belief in moderation. So when a leader seemed to be disrupting the harmony by making inordinate demands, a concerned citizen could write his name on a piece of broken pottery (an *ostracon*) and drop it into a large container near the Pnyx. Special meetings were held during which the *ostraca* were removed and examined. If the name of a man appeared on 6,000 *ostraca*, he was banished (ostracized) from the city for ten years. After that period of time, he could return to Athens as though nothing had happened. Today, the word "ostracize" means "to exclude a person from a group or society."

ostraca

In the 70 years that this system was used, only 10 men were ostracized. Hundreds of *ostraca* have since been found in archaeological excavations. The names of some of the greatest leaders of the Golden Age were written upon these pottery fragments. Even then, no one could please all the people all the time.

Pericles

About twenty years after the Persian Wars ended, the Strategoi selected as Commander-in-Chief a man of outstanding ability who would leave his mark upon their city. This was Pericles, a statesman, orator (public speaker) and military leader. He was the great nephew of Cleisthenes, and he governed for over thirty years (460-429 B.C.E.). Pericles was annually elected during that period by the Ecclesia, and so his power came directly from the people. Yet, his brilliance, charisma and sense of vision enabled him to personally mold the major policies of Athens during the three decades he was in power.

Pericles

Pericles was proud of Athens' rich heritage, and he believed that the city should set a shining example for the rest of Greece. During his terms of office, he encouraged artists, writers, and scientists to come to what was rapidly becoming the intellectual and creative center of the Greek world.

Pericles loosened some of the financial requirements for citizenship and saw to it that those who served in government were paid for their services. Now a merchant could afford to serve at court or attend a meeting of the Ecclesia or the Boule without sacrificing any of his income. As a result, official policies were no longer based solely upon the interests of the wealthy elite. Athens could proudly boast that every citizen was the master of his own person and an active participant in his city's government.

The long walls connecting Athens to Piraeus

A Corridor to the Sea

One of Pericles' first goals was to fortify Athens against foreign invasion. A long wooden palisade already encircled the Acropolis (remember the wooden walls?) and a twenty-foot high stone wall surrounded the entire city. But Athens lay five miles inland from the sea, and Pericles worried that an enemy could easily surround and besiege the city, cutting off the food supply. After carefully studying the local landscape, he ordered the construction of two long stone walls (about 500 feet apart) stretching from Athens to the harbor of Piraeus. The walls would provide a safe corridor through which food could be delivered from ships

moored at Piraeus. Since the Athenian fleet ruled the high seas, the corridor seemed to insure Athens' survival in the most trying of circumstances.

Once the city seemed secure, Pericles turned his attention to the buildings themselves. After the Persians sacked and burned Athens, new structures of mud-brick had been built on the site. But Pericles envisioned something grander. It was he who quietly withdrew some of the Delian funds to hire the best artists and architects in Greece. Under his guidance, plans were made for the construction of elegant marble temples, majestic government buildings, and graceful colonnades around the *agora* (marketplace).

The Acropolis

The Athenian Acropolis, once the site of a Mycenean citadel, rose dramatically 260 feet above the city. Since Dorian days it had been the spiritual center of Athens, the site of several temples dedicated to the city's patron goddess, Athena. Pericles decided that the time was right to level everything left standing on the hilltop in order to construct the finest temples the people of the ancient world had ever seen. The temples would lavishly honor Athena, and the Acropolis would become an awe-inspiring symbol of the city's power and greatness.

As we have learned, the design of a typical Greek temple was simple yet elegant. Its rectangular structure was surrounded by tall graceful pillars that supported a pitched roof and formed a colonnade (columned porch) around the outer edges of the building. There were a series of low steps on every side. The triangular gables at the front and back of the building are called

Corinthian   Ionic   Doric

Three types of columns

The Parthenon

The most impressive temple built on the Acropolis was the Parthenon (it derives its name from *Athena Parthenos*, which means "Athena the Maiden.") Pericles commissioned the architects Ictinus and Callicrates to design the building, and its actual construction required fourteen years.

Today the ruins of the Parthenon still dominate the hilltop above the modern bustling city of Athens. Its very dimensions are imposing. It is 228 feet long, 101 feet wide and 65 feet high. Originally the building had a wooden roof covered with clay tiles, but this was destroyed in the seventeenth century.

pediments. A temple's entrance always faced east, so that the rays of the morning sun could fall upon the statue of the god or goddess that stood in the inner sanctuary.

The concept of columns possibly came from Egypt, where beautiful stone pillars had been used for millennia. There are several styles of Greek column. They differ mainly in the design of the capital (the top section). The Doric column has a simple capital which reflects the primitive, down-to-earth Dorian culture. It was the most popular type of column in mainland Greece. The graceful Ionic column came from the artistic people of Ionia and was popular there and on the Aegean Islands. Its capital appears to be framed with a set of curled ram's horns. The elaborate Corinthian column became popular after the Golden Age, and it seems to convey the somewhat ostentatious nature of the merchants of Corinth. Its capital is decorated with acanthus leaves. It was not used very often in ancient Greece, but later it became very popular with the Romans.

Fluted Doric columns once supported the roof. Seventeen columns flank each side of the building, while eight extend across the front and rear walls. The vertical lines of fluting cut into the stone trap long shadows, which make the columns appear slender and graceful. The Greeks understood how the physical world can play tricks on the human eye, creating an optical illusion. For this reason, the architects designed columns that bulge in the center, taper at the top and lean slightly inward. Had the columns been built perfectly straight, they would have appeared to be leaning outward from their bases; given their actual design, they look straight and tall when viewed from a distance. There is no trace of the paint that once embellished the columns, but the white marble contains veins of iron that give the building a golden glow at dawn and dusk.

The wide marble steps leading up to the front of the Parthenon are higher in the center than they are on the sides. Here again, the architects compensated for the effects of an optical illusion. If the wide steps were completely level, a person observing from a distance would have thought that the entire temple and its stairway sagged dramatically in the middle.

The triangular pediments on the front and rear gables of the temple were originally decorated with free-standing sculptures. Unfortunately, most of the statues have disappeared, but descriptions of them that

The ruins of the Parthenon

The temple was decorated with relief figures (cut into a stone background) and free-standing sculptures that were designed by Phidias, the very same man who created the giant statue of Zeus in Olympia. A band of carved marble runs along the top of the outer walls of the temple. This is called a frieze. It is 520 feet long and a little more than three feet high. The carvings depict a procession of young Athenian men, some on horseback and others leading sheep and cows to be sacrificed to Athena at the concluding ceremonies of the Panathenaic Games. Also represented in the procession are maidens and government magistrates, and in one section there is a group of seated Olympian gods who seem to be viewing the parading figures with great interest.

were written centuries ago give us an idea of what they must have looked like in the days of Pericles. Those figures over the main entrance represented the birth of Athena (remember that Athena sprang fully armed from the head of Zeus). The sculptures on the rear pediment portrayed the contest between Athena and Poseidon (each wanted to be the patron deity of Athens). According to Greek myth, Poseidon thrust his trident into a rock and water flowed down to the sea. He then promised to bring the city riches through sea trade if he was chosen patron god. (In another version of the myth he offered the horse.) Athena's offering was an olive tree. The people of the city considered the olive tree more useful than Poseidon's water, and so they made Athena their patron goddess.

Modern replica of the Parthenon

Religious ceremonies for the public were held at altars placed outside the temple. The interior of the building was the home of the deity, and it was reserved for private prayers by priests and privileged citizens. A majestic forty-foot high statue of Athena, sculpted by Phidias in gold and ivory around a wooden core, once stood in one of the two inner chambers of the Parthenon. The crown upon her head nearly brushed the ceiling. Phidias designed the statue so that the gold plating could be removed and weighed in order to prove that he had used every ounce of gold delivered to him. Even then, the government officials were suspicious of their employees. This magnificent statue disappeared centuries ago, but we know of its existence because it is carefully described in the works of Greek historians. The other temple chamber was a treasury, once holding the funds of the Delian League.

A detailed guidebook written by Pausanias, a Greek traveler of the second century C.E. (the same man who described the Mycenean grave-stones), enabled modern archaeologists to discover the actual studio of Phidias. Among the ruins of the workshop lay many of the tools and terra-cotta molds once used by that great artist.

Other Temples on the Acropolis

The Acropolis was also the site of several smaller temples of great beauty. The Erechtheum was built on the north side of the hilltop. It was named for Erechtheus, a legendary ancestor of the city's Mycenean kings. On the south side of the temple is the small Porch of the Maidens. The roof is supported by Caryatids (carved stone maidens) instead of traditional columns. Caryatids are named for the women of Caryae.

A small temple dedicated to Athena Nike (nike means "victory" or "victorious") was built to commemorate the Greek victory

The porch of the maidens

over the Persians. The frieze on the outer walls depicts one of the battles of the Persian Wars. The Propylaea is a ceremonial gateway to the Acropolis. It is a curious mixture of Doric and Ionic marble columns. The stone dramatically changes color throughout the day, varying from gold and honey in the early hours to rose and gray toward dusk. Not far from the Propylaea was once a huge bronze statue of Athena: The crest of her helmet and the point of her spear could be seen by sailors entering the distant harbor at Pireaus.

Advances in Sculpture

The sculptures of the temples of the Acropolis give us an idea of the great advances made by the Greek artists since the Archaic period. While the earlier figures were stiff and unnatural, those of the Golden Age are extremely life-like representations of handsome men and women. These statues are remarkable for their beauty and grace as well as the feeling of quiet restraint that they convey. And they bear witness to the genius of the Greeks, who could create

harmony and order out of a formless block of stone—just as Gaea and Uranus once molded Cosmos out of Chaos.

Another gifted sculptor of the Golden Age was Polyclitus, an artist with a knack for mathematics. He worked out a mathematical formula for the physical dimensions of a statue: the figure was divided into seven sections, each equal to the size of its head. These were further subdivided into sections

Marble statue of a Greek woman

the size of a palm. For example, the lower leg from the foot to the kneecap was three palms. His precise formula was followed by most classical sculptors who came after him.

Greek statues were used to decorate not only temples but private homes as well. They were also made to commemorate the lives of famous people and to mark graves. Although most of the statues have disappeared, a fair number have survived for us to appreciate. Many broken works of art have been recovered from the soil of the Acropolis itself. Others have been discovered at the bottom of the sea, often aboard ancient sunken merchant ships that capsized in storms. A beautiful bronze statue of Poseidon was found beneath the waters of the Aegean. This seems an appropriate place to find the god of the sea! Fortunately, the Roman artists were so impressed with the Greek sculptures that they made numerous copies of them, and many of these have often survived the ravages of time when the Greek originals have not.

Pottery

The clay vases and jugs molded by Greek potters are an important source of information about life in those early times. Vessels of many shapes and sizes are decorated with paintings of Olympic athletes, the heroes and monsters of Homer's epics, and scenes of everyday Athenian life. The vases made during the sixth century B.C.E. have black figures against a red (orange) background, while those of the fifth century are the reverse (red figures against a black background). The coloration of the pottery depends upon the method by which it was fired. There was a particular

district in Athens where the potters had their workshops. It was called Ceramicus, and this is the source of our word "ceramics".

Greek vase, red figures on black

Greek vase, black figures on red

Drama

One of the most important achievements of the Golden Age was in drama. Theater as we know it was invented by the Greeks, and the art of playwriting blossomed in the fifth century. The earliest plays grew out of impromptu forms of entertainment at religious festivals. The Festival of Dionysus was held each spring in Athens to mark the budding of the leaves of the grapevine (sacred to the wine god). During the festivities, local men donned goatskins and dressed as satyrs (mythical creatures, half man and half goat). They gaily danced around a statue of Dionysus, while a chorus sang about the exploits and achievements of the god to the accompaniment of a double flute and drum. From this simple beginning, Greek tragic drama slowly evolved into a sophisticated art form. Actually, the word tragedy comes from the Greek word *tragoedia* meaning "goat song".

Tradition credits the poet Thespis (from the island of Icaria) with first providing lines for a single member of the chorus to recite in response to those of the rest of the group. Today, the word thespian means "actor." Eventually, other writers produced plays in which two or three soloists conversed among themselves, and the role of the chorus was gradually reduced to simply providing background information about the actions being portrayed or discussed by the soloists. Music was an important part of a theatrical performance, and many lines were sung to the accompaniment of a flute.

The Great Playwrights

The tragedies that were written during the Golden Age often dealt with the rather strained relations between human beings and the Olympic gods and goddesses, and they focused upon the difficulties of trying to lead a good life.

Aeschylus (525–456 B.C.E.) was the first of three great playwrights of tragedies (tragedians) of the Golden Age. He had been a soldier at Marathon and Salamis, and as a young man he wrote a play entitled *The Persians*. (His producer was the young Pericles himself.). His later works are based upon Greek myths and legends, and they deal with the agony experienced by an individual caught in a conflict. *The Orestia* is a trilogy about three generations of the family of King Agamemnon of Mycenae.

The second playwright was Sophocles (496–406 B.C.E.). His name means "the wise and honored one." Like many Greek scholars, he was intrigued by the complexity of the human mind. He once said that the world is full of wonders, but nothing is more wonderful than man. Yet, man has his faults. Sophocles observed that a superabundance of one trait, such as envy or pride (the much dreaded *hubris*), upset a natural balance and caused a person's downfall. The prophetic words, "Nothing in excess," inscribed on the wall of Apollo's temple long before, remained the motto of every educated Greek, and those who ignored this call for restraint were "out of sync" with the ideals of classical society.

The plays of Sophocles depict people who are victimized by a lack of balance in their

Sophocles

characters or in their lives; they struggle valiantly but hopelessly against forces that are greater than themselves. Sophocles wrote 113 plays, but only seven have survived. Two of his most popular works are *Antigone* and *Oedipus*.

The works of Euripides (480–406 B.C.E.), the last of the "big three tragedians" of Athens, often concern a person who brings ruin upon himself (and usually his family as well) because he allows his emotions to master his powers of reason. His most powerful play, *Medea*, is based upon the story of Jason and the Golden Fleece.

It has been said that while Sophocles saw men as they ought to be (his main characters are heroic), Euripides saw men as they actually are. Euripides was also critical of the traditional Greek religion, and he described the long-worshipped Olympian gods as cruel, deceitful and immoral beings who were not worthy of respect.

In contrast to tragedies, Greek comedies were light-hearted, often irreverent plays that poked fun at human weaknesses and mocked many aspects of everyday life and politics. Often the names of people sitting in the audience—even generals and statesmen— were included in a frolicsome episode. The greatest of the comic poets was Aristophanes (445–385 B.C.E.)

Thousands of plays (comedies and tragedies) were written by the ancient Greeks. Although most of them have been lost, thirty-three have survived relatively intact, and these are still produced and enjoyed by modern audiences. The intricacy of the human soul and the difficulties that arise when individuals are brought into conflict with each other or with the fates are timeless subjects that will always intrigue the minds of thoughtful people.

The Theater

The Greeks invented the open air theater for the production of their plays. After the temples of the Acropolis had been rebuilt, Pericles ordered the construction of the huge theater of Dionysus on the south slope of the famous hilltop. (Dionysus thus became the god of the theater as well as the divinity of wine.)

The stone seats of the amphitheater were arranged in a semi-circle. They accommodated 18,000 people. The front rows were reserved for the priests of Dionysus, government officials, and other guests of honor. At the bottom of the slope was a circular area (called the *orchestra*) where the chorus stood. Beyond the orchestra was a raised stage (the *proscenium*). Behind it was a long building (the *skene*) which served as a dressing room. The wall of the *skene* facing the audience could be decorated as a background for the play being presented

Ruins of the theater of Dionysus

Ruins of the Theater of Epidaurus

on the stage. This is the origin of our word "scene".

Behind the *skene* was a crane with pulley and weights. It was used to transport an actor through the air when he was playing the role of a god or goddess. This device was called a *mechane* (machine); the Romans later called the sudden appearance of a deity by this means *deus ex machina* ("a god transported by the machine"). The Latin phrase is still used today to describe an artificial or miraculous event written into a play to solve a thorny problem in the plot.

The Greeks also had some other ingenious special effects. For example, they created the sound of thunder by propelling large round rocks through a tunnel built under the seats of the audience. The thunder claps must have been startling to those sitting just above the tunnel.

The acoustics of the open-air theaters were remarkably effective. At the ancient theater of Epidaurus on the Peloponnese, the voice of a person standing on the stage can be clearly heard in the very last row. This restored theater is currently used for annual drama festivals.

Front row seats

The performers of the Golden Age were professional actors who were paid by the state. Men played the male as well as female parts, since women were not allowed to participate in theatricals. The actors were held in high esteem by the people, and they were even exempt from military service. The Greek word for actor is *hypocrites*, and our word hypocrite is derived from it. Like an actor, a hypocrite pretends to be something that he isn't.

The Greek actors wore padded clothes and ten-inch platform shoes to make them appear "larger than life." They often wore masks made of stiffened linen, the mouths of which were shaped like megaphones to amplify their voices. The facial expression of a mask worn for a tragedy was sorrowful, while a comic mask had a laughing face. Special masks were worn to represent female characters.

Going to the theater in Athens was an all-day affair, since many plays (usually three tragedies and a comedy) were presented together at a single performance. The plays at the Festival of Dionysus were presented over a period of three days. A theatergoer took along a box lunch to consume during an interval between plays. He also probably carried along a soft pillow to sit upon (remember, the seats were of stone). During such a festival all business was suspended, law courts were closed, and prisoners were even released from their cells. Tickets to the plays were inexpensive, and those people who could not afford them had their way paid by the state, since theater-going was considered a civic as well as a religious activity. What better way was there to celebrate Greece's cultural heritage?

Since the plays were based upon well-known myths and legends, everyone in the audience knew the stories. What interested the crowd was the manner in which a play was presented. The audience openly displayed approval or disapproval of a production by stamping their feet, shouting at the actors, or cheering boisterously. Occasionally they threw rocks and vegetables to indicate their displeasure.

In earliest times the writer of the best tragic trilogy was given a goat, while the best comedy won its author a jug of wine and a basket of figs. By the Golden Age, the prizes were usually a Dionysian wreath of grapevine or a sum of money. They were awarded at the end of the performances to the best producer, the best actor, and the best playwright. Sophocles won first prize at the festival twenty times.

Mask for a tragedy

Poets and Historians

Music and poetry were closely related. The poets of the late Archaic Age had broken with the heroic tradition of Homer and begun to write about themselves— their loves, their sorrows and their hopes. Following in this tradition of self-expression, the poets of the Golden Age wrote many beautiful and evocative descriptions of basic human emotions. Because these works were recited or chanted to the accompaniment of a lyre, they are called lyric poetry. Today, we use this term to describe expressive poems dealing with human emotional experiences. Men called rhapsodes often recited poetry (rhapsodies) at religious festivals.

We have already heard a great deal about Herodotus, the Father of History. He was born in Halicarnasus (just south of Ionia) in 485 B.C.E. Like most of the Greeks of his time, Herodotus was extremely curious about the nature of the world. He asked many questions and thoroughly investigated matters that he didn't understand. As a young man he traveled widely, visiting Egypt, Phoenicia and Babylon and taking copious notes about the customs and historical events of the local areas. Unlike Homer, Herodotus dealt only with the real and the factual. He once remarked, "the stories of the Greeks (of earlier centuries) are numerous, and, in my opinion, ridiculous!"

Herodotus carefully studied the geography of the lands he visited, for he believed that the natural environment strongly influenced the development of a culture. On his visit to Egypt, for example, he ascended the Nile River to the First Cataract (a series of rapids) and wrote a detailed description of the landscape.

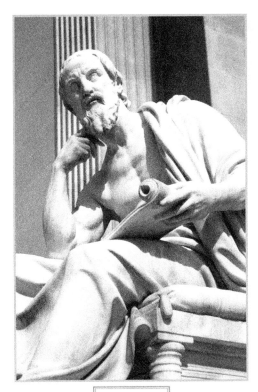

Herodotus

Herodotus later settled in Athens, where he wrote his great work, *The History* (the Greek word *historia* means "an inquiry"). This massive volume is a thoughtful study of Greek civilization, centering upon the period of the Persian Wars. It also includes a scholarly analysis of the rise of the Persian Empire, a colorful description of the contrasting cultures of Athens and Sparta, and a lively commentary on the customs of the Egyptians and the Scythians (people living in western Asia).

The History is the oldest surviving study of its kind, and as such it is an invaluable source of data relating to the ancient world. Although he was frequently so caught up by his enthusiasm for his subject that he exaggerated many of his descriptions, Herodotus was the first scholar to separate history from legend, basing his writings upon established facts. In the opening lines of his work, he wrote of the importance of making a record of the times "so that past deeds will not be forgotten through the lapse of time." Thanks to him, our knowledge of those past deeds is greater than it would otherwise have been.

Exciting Times

The Golden Age of Athens must have been an exhilarating time to live. Imagine being a witness to the explosion of creativity that had been building up for so many centuries, when Athens became the artistic, intellectual, and cultural center of the Mediterrtanean world. But how long could it last?

Questions

1. What was the original purpose of the Delian League?

2. Why did many of the members of the League begin to resent Athens?

3. What were the qualifications for citizenship?

4. What were the three branches of the Greek government?

5. What is ostracism?

6. Why did Pericles build a wall?

7. Describe the frieze of the Parthenon.

8. How did Greek drama originate?

9. Describe a Greek theater.

10. What are the strengths and weaknesses of Herodotus' works?

Further Thoughts

1. The island of Delos, sacred to Apollo (it was his birthplace), was so hallowed that no one was allowed to be born or to die there. Therefore, all pregnant women and sick people were taken across a narrow channel to another island, Rhenea.

2. Themistocles, the hero of the Battle of Salamis during the Persian Wars, oversaw the building of the walls of Athens. In 471 B.C.E. he was ostracized, and so he settled in the city of Argos. He was later accused of treason (he apparently spoke against the alliance with Sparta and was too closely associated with the Persians). And so he moved on, this time to Anatolia, where the Persian King Artaxerxes (who was grateful to him for helping to negotiate peace with Athens after the war) made him governor of three cities. Themistocles lived well until he was sixty-five. Some scholars believe he then ended his own life. (Did he pine for his homeland?)

3. The olive tree, sacred to Athena and the symbol of her city, was a source of Athenian commercial wealth. It is a stately tree with a thick grey trunk and lovely green leaves whose silver backs are revealed in a gentle breeze. It requires sixteen years to mature and forty years to reach its peak production of fruit. This being so, it is not surprising that Pericles declared it a criminal offense to uproot or cut down an olive tree.

4. The Parthenon survived relatively intact for nearly two thousand years. When Athena was no longer worshipped, the building was used as a Christian church and, more recently, as a Muslim mosque. The Turks later made the temple a storehouse for gunpowder. In 1687 Italian soldiers besieged some Turks who were quartered on the Acropolis; the Italians threw a grenade-like device that exploded and destroyed the inside structures of the ancient temple as well as the roof. An earthquake in a later

century further contributed to the crumbling of some of the outer walls. It is a tragedy that an insignificant battle in modern times could substantially damage a magnificent building that had endured nearly intact for centuries.

5. A Roman historian named Vetruvius wrote that the Caryatids fought with the Persians at the battle of Salamis against the Greeks. After the Greeks won the battle, they destroyed the city of the Caryatids. They killed all the men and brought the women back to Athens as slaves. Greek sculptors copied the Caryatid slave women in stone, forcing them to carry the roof of the Erectheum on their heads for eternity. Today, a column in the shape of a woman is called a caryatid, while one depicting a man is an atlas.

Two of the Elgin Marbles

6. Early in the nineteenth century, Lord Elgin of Great Britain "rescued" parts of a frieze of the Parthenon, sculptures from the pediment, and one of the Caryatids of the porch of the Erectheum. They are now in the British Museum and are referred to as the Elgin Marbles. Many people feel that they should be returned to Athens. Indeed, it is now a law that any artifacts discovered on Greek soil must be given to local authorities and displayed in Greek museums.

7. Although their tragedies often contain references to violent acts, the Greeks considered it inappropriate to have these acts take place upon the stage. For this reason, characters were always wounded or murdered off-stage. The audience would simply hear the screams of the victim! There were two doors at the middle of the wall of the skene. After an offstage murder, the doors would open and a platform on wheels (an eccyclema) carried out the draped body of "the deceased" for the audience to see.

8. Herodotus wasn't the first Greek to look beyond the mythological explanations of life posed by his ancestors. In the sixth century B.C.E. Hecataeus of Miletus had tried to describe as accurately as possible the events of the past.

Projects

1. The division of our government into three branches (legislative, executive and judicial) has its origins in the democracy of ancient Athens. Find out more about the functions of the three branches in American government; then compare and contrast them with their counterparts in Athens. Using poster board, make a chart comparing the two systems of government.

2. Greek architectural styles are evident throughout our country. Look at the buildings in your city. Pay particular attention to government buildings and stately mansions. What kinds of pillars do you see (Doric, Ionic or Corinthian)? Look through magazines and clip pictures of buildings that show a Greek influence. Make a collage of the pictures.

3. Sappho was a Greek poetess from the island of Lesbos. Her poignant odes and poems reflect her ideas about such human emotions as love and friendship. Find out more about her and her works. Present a report to the class. Quote a few lines from her poems, if possible.

4. A Greek slave named Aesop is credited with the creation of many fables that are read to this very day. These include the stories of the tortoise and the hare and the fox and the crow. Read a collection of Aesop's fables and make a report to the class.

5. Read a tragedy by Aeschylus, Sophocles or Euripides and a comedy by Aristophanes. The greatest of the comedies is *The Clouds*. Write a short report explaining why these plays, written so long ago, have a strong appeal for modern audiences.

6. Here is how a Greek artist made a mask for the theater: He put olive oil on the face of the actor, then lay narrow strips of linen around his head, leaving openings for his eyes, nostrils and mouth; then other strips were dipped in a paste made from flour and water and placed criss-cross over the first ones; after about ten minutes, he cut through the strips at the back of the actor's head and removed it. He could then build up the nose and other facial features by adding more linen and then smoothing it over with plaster. After the mask dried, he painted it and then coated it with a substance like varnish.

7. You can make your own mask with your teacher following these steps, but with some variations. Using a combination of strips of bandage or paper and glue made from flour and water, shape your mask on the face of a friend or else over the outside of a glass bowl. Remove it, and when it is dry, decorate it. Use the mask to put on an original play.

Ruins of the Acropolis in Athens

CHAPTER 12

THE SPARTAN WAY OF LIFE

While Athens sparkled, Sparta remained a dour stronghold of the military ways of Dorian times. Any spirit of creativity and experimentation had been permanently stifled after the rebellion of the Messenians. Sparta's identity was wrapped up with its valiant soldiers, who protected their city "in the place of walls or bricks." They certainly proved themselves to be superior fighters in the Persian Wars. Given their reputation, it is clear why no other city-state would even think of attacking Sparta.

Spartan Society

The Spartan government stood in stark contrast to those of the democratic city-states. It was ruled by two kings, who commanded the army in times of war and conducted religious ceremonies. In all other matters, the government was run by a group of five overseers (called the *Ephors*) who were elected annually. A Council of Elders made up of men over 60 (they served for life) advised the *Ephors* and performed as judges. A large Assembly was open to all citizens over 30, but its members' powers were very limited. They simply voted on matters previously discussed by the *Ephors* by shouting yes or no—the group that shouted loudest won.

We have already learned how the Spartans depended upon the labor of the *helots*, an enslaved people who out-numbered them seven to one. The *helots* were treated harshly. They were beaten if they did not

An original Spartan helmet

Modern Sparta lies beyond the ruins of the ancient polis

produce sufficient crops, and they could be put to death if they complained. All *helots* had to be home by dusk, and no lights were allowed in their villages during the hours of darkness. Groups of young Spartan soldiers patrolled the streets at night with knives, killing any *helots* who weren't in their houses. Spartan society was divided into three groups: *Spartiates* (citizens), *mothakes* (non-Spartan free men raised as Spartans), and *perioikoi* (craftsmen who lived on the outskirts of the city).

A Soldier's Life

From the moment of birth, a Spartan citizen's life was determined and molded by the army. A newborn baby was inspected by the Council of Elders. If they considered the child frail or abnormal in any way, it was abandoned on a hillside to die. They believed that only strong, healthy baby boys could become fine soldiers, just as only robust girls could become the mothers of future warriors.

Spartan boys lived at home until they were seven, when they were sent off to military camp. There they were taught by older soldiers to obey orders without questioning them. The boys consumed a sparse amount of food, wore the skimpiest of clothing (they ran barefoot, even in the snow), and slept outside on piles of rushes in all kinds of weather. Every ten days they were lined up and examined to make sure they weren't getting fat. They exercised constantly, and they learned to fight and to endure hardship without complaining. Emotion was considered a sign of weakness, and a Spartan lad often bit his lip to stifle a cry of pain. Whipping contests were held at the camps to determine who could stand the most pain without crying. Occasionally a boy would die rather than beg for an end to the lashes.

Sometimes the boys were given no food at all, so that they would learn to live off the land. They were even encouraged to steal, since a soldier's survival might depend upon his ability to obtain food in this way. A boy was punished if he was caught stealing, not because of the theft itself but because he had gotten caught. According to legend, a Spartan boy once hid a stolen fox under his tunic—when confronted by his teachers, he let the creature rip his chest open rather than admit to his theft. Another common camp activity was a stealing competition. The boys had to try to steal pieces of cheese while dodging blows from their teachers' whips.

At the age of twenty a young man lived and trained in an army barracks. He was given a portion of land by the state and a number of *helots* to work it and produce

A Spartan warrior

his food. (The *helots* were allowed to keep a small amount of what they grew.) This left the Spartan free to pursue his military career. At the age of twenty-eight he was eligible to serve in the front line of the army.

Any man who married before the age of 30 had to visit his wife and children in secret. Yet, if he did not marry by the age of 38 he was punished, and street gangs of women beat up uncommitted bachelors. But once married, a soldier continued to spend his time at the barracks; only old men actually lived with their wives in their own houses.

For the Spartans, then, the military life was the only life, and they focused all their energy into becoming invincible fighters. It was said that a Spartan soldier was worth at least ten of any other Greek *hoplite*. He was easily recognized by his long hair and his red cloak, and a steadily advancing line of red-cloaked fighters must have put fear into the hearts of any opposing army.

A Spartan was trained to fight to the death rather than retreat (remember the courageous stand of Leonidas at Thermopylae). A Spartan mother once told her son to return from battle either with his shield or on it. The meaning of the message is clear: A coward would drop his heavy and cumbersome shield before deserting his post, while a heroic warrior would hold it until the moment of his death. After a battle, the bodies of slain soldiers were placed upon their shields and carried home by their comrades.

A Conservative Polis

The Spartans resisted change of any kind, because they feared that new ideas might weaken their strict regulations and thereby threaten their absolute control of the *helots*. In fact, most foreigners were not even allowed in Sparta. Spartan citizens were sometimes called *homoioi,* which means "men who are similar." There was no room for individuality in that harsh *polis*. And just as boys had to obey their teachers, soldiers displayed absolute obedience to command on the battlefield.

Thanks to the work done by the *helots* and the *perioikoi*, Sparta was able to remain self-sufficient. There was no trade with other city-states, and the currency used throughout the rest of Greece had no value in Sparta. Local products were simply exchanged (bartered), although sometimes iron bars were used to represent specific amounts.

The Spartans had no time for reading and writing, since every moment had to be utilized for military procedures. Their simple life style became proverbial. (Today the word "spartan" means extremely self-disciplined or self-retrained.) Music was encouraged, however, because it was useful for the soldiers to march to a rhythm.

And so while Athens experienced a flowering of art and drama, the Spartans remained close-minded and illiterate. These city-states, opposite in so many ways, remained the two major powers in Greece for a long time.

Questions

1. Who were the Ephors?

2. Why did the Spartans believe that they needed to have a strong military state?

3. Describe the daily life of a Spartan teenage boy.

4. What does it mean to return home "either with your shield or on it"?

5. How was a Spartan soldier recognized?

Further Thoughts

1. Spartan girls were encouraged to participate in sports alongside the boys so that they would be strong, healthy mothers. In this respect, they had greater opportunities to interact with young men than did their counterparts in the other city-states. Not surprisingly, the Athenians belittled the Spartan women and considered them uncouth. In Sparta childbirth was considered the female equivalent of battle. In fact, the only Spartans honored in marked tombs were men killed in battle and women who died in childbirth.

2. A Spartan who didn't fight bravely was called a "trembler." He was forced to shave one side of his face and to keep a beard on the other. He was thus easily identifiable as the target of scorn and ridicule in his city.

3. Spartan food was often mocked by other Greeks. Most unappetizing of all was the famous Spartan black broth made from pork cooked in blood, vinegar and salt. An Athenian once tasted this watery stew and then remarked that he finally understood why Spartans were so willing to die.

4. Sparta lies in the region of Laconia. As we have learned, the Spartans prided themselves on "roughing it," existing with few material comforts and wasting nothing. This philosophy also applied to the spoken word. Today, the word "laconic" means "expressing much in a few words" (concise). Here is an historic example of a laconic remark. When king Philip of Macedonia invaded Greece (more about him later), he hoped that the Spartans would not become involved in his battles against the other Greek city-states. If they did not stay put, he would have to invade their polis. Philip sent a messenger to Sparta to deliver a challenge that ended with the following words; "If we invade your city, we will raze it to the ground!" The Spartan reply was, quite simply, "If!"

Projects

1. On poster board make a chart that compares and contrasts the systems of government in Athens and Sparta.

2. If you are a girl, would you prefer to have lived in Athens or Sparta? Give specific reasons for your choice.

3. The Spartans continued the ways of the Dorians. Write a paragraph describing how the Spartans perpetuated the life style of the warriors who conquered the Myceneans.

4. Can you think of a modern person or society that has a spartan lifestyle? Is it by choice or circumstances? Write a paragraph about the advantages of living with only the bare essentials.

5. The Spartans claimed that their unique way of life originated with a man named Lycurgus, who lived around 850 B.C.E. He established the government of Kings and Ephors. Find out more about Lycurgus and write a short report.

6. The Spartans highly valued tradition and discipline. They believed the Athenian pursuit of individual freedom led to disorder and decline in morality. Do you see any sign of these opposing political views in modern politics? Explain.

CHAPTER 13

Daily Life in Athens

The spirit of Athens during the Golden Age was one of optimism and supreme confidence. People of every walk of life enjoyed expressing their views, attending public performances, and taking advantage of the rich variety of products brought into their city every day. Wealth was distributed fairly evenly among the upper class, and even members of the lower classes lived quite comfortably.

A small street in modern Greece looks a lot like a street in ancient times.

Athenian Dwellings

The typical Athenian house stood beside a crooked, narrow street paved with cobblestones. It was constructed of sun-dried mud bricks laid over a framework of wooden beams on a stone base. It was designed to keep the family cool during the long hot summer and warm in the winter. The outer surface of the dwelling was covered with stucco (a plaster made of sand and crushed stone). The walls were often so soft that burglars could easily cut through them, which explains why the Greek word for burglars (*toichorychoi*) literally means "wall diggers." The pitched roof was covered with overlapping clay tiles. Near the main entrance of the house stood a statue of Hermes (called a Herm) whose main function was to ward off evil.

There were few windows facing the street. Family life centered around an inner open-air courtyard where flowers bloomed in the bright sunshine. An altar stood in the courtyard, usually dedicated to the goddess Hestia (goddess of the household). Slender columns surrounded the courtyard and supported the sloping roof. This encircling colonnade provided the family with shade in hot weather and shelter on rainy days.

Facing on the courtyard were the kitchen, bathroom (with a large bathtub could be filled with water from the well or public fountain), and the men's dining area (the *andron*). A storeroom held large storage jars called *amphorae* and *pithoi*, which were filled with olive oil, wine, and grain (which could be ground into flour). There might be a workroom, where slaves would perform tasks like making shoes or jewelry. Bedrooms were usually on a second level, although more modest dwellings had only one floor. The woman of the house had separate quarters—a large room called the *gynaeceum*, where she could spin, weave, and entertain her friends. This is where the wife of an Athenian citizen spent most of her life. The inner walls of the dwelling of a wealthy family were often decorated with fresco paintings.

A Greek home had a sparse amount of furniture by modern standards—a few tables, chairs, beds and couches. But each piece was carefully carved and decorated by a skilled craftsman. The wealthy Athenians owned furnishings made of beautiful imported wood, such as red cedar from Lebanon and black ebony from Africa. These handsome pieces were often inlaid with gold, silver or ivory. The *thronus* was a huge armchair used by the head of a well-to-do family (a very wealthy man might have one made of marble). In humbler residences the head of the family sat upon a simpler wooden armchair with a leather seat, his feet resting upon a footstool. A *klismos* was a straight-backed chair with no arms that was used by a guest of honor (and, at private family gatherings, by the woman of the house). Everyone else sat on plain stools that folded up for easy storage.

A bed and a dining couch were important pieces of furniture that had a similar design. Each consisted of a wooden frame strung with leather thongs upon which was placed a mattress and pillows. The couch was used by the man of the family, who reclined to eat his main meal of the day, leaning on the pillows with one arm while helping himself to food with the other. Dining tables were often three-legged, and they were low so that they could be tucked under couches when they were not needed.

The Greeks used wooden boxes of all sizes for the storage of spare clothing, blankets

Reclining while dining

and armor, since there were no closets or even shelves in their homes. Some everyday items, such as cups, baskets, and cloaks, were hung on metal hooks attached to the plaster walls. Room lighting was provided at night by a metal or pottery lamp containing olive oil and a wick (it must have been very dim). Charcoal was burned in small portable metal braziers for heat during the winter months. Most of the smoke went out through a hole in the roof.

The household slaves obtained water for the family at a local spring, although a few wealthy citizens had private wells dug on their property. Clay pipes conducted dirty water from the bathrooms into an open drain that ran down the center of the street. Garbage was often thrown into the street, where it was eaten by wandering dogs and rodents. Chamber pots, kept in the bedrooms, were also dumped into a gutter in the street. Small wonder that the living quarters of the house faced away from the smelly roadways and toward the pleasant inner courtyard.

How the Greeks Dressed

An Athenian man's everyday garment was a rectangular piece of wool woven by his wife. It was called a *chiton*. To get dressed, he simply wrapped the material loosely around his body and fastened it with a pin at one or both shoulders (depending on the latest fashion). The garment fell in folds to his

A chiton in sculpture

Apollo models a chiton

lower thigh. It was gathered at the waist with a leather cord. Short sleeves could be fashioned by gathering and pinning some of the material at the upper arm. (Long sleeves were the sign of a slave or workman, and an Athenian citizen wouldn't dream of having them.) The *chiton* was also the basic garment of Greek women, but theirs were ankle-length. Greek men generally wore light-colored or bleached white chitons (often decorated with a narrow border), while the women preferred material that was dyed and patterned with bright colors. Beginning in the fifth century B.C.E. some wealthy Greeks wore *chitons* made from cotton that was imported from India. Egyptian linen was another popular material for the summer months.

Greek men never wore trousers. Indeed, they considered them the mark of a barbarian. The standard footwear was the leather sandal, although most people went barefoot in the privacy of their homes.

A long cloak, called a *himation*, was often draped over one's *chiton* in cool weather. There was an art to draping a *himation*, and people who did not do it properly quickly became the object of ridicule. To do it right, one end of the cloak was placed at the waist under the right arm, the material was thrown over the left shoulder, pulled under the right arm, and then tossed over the left shoulder again. If the loose end was too long it would drag in the mud, and if it was too short, it would just look silly. A shorter cloak, called a *chlamlys*, was often worn by younger men.

The average Greek did not possess many articles of clothing, and so he had to take good care of what he had. Clothing thieves roamed the cities, and they were quick to grab a *chiton* or *himation* left unattended while its owner was bathing or exercising.

A well-draped himation

A chiton could be cleaned by a worker called a fuller. He made a paste from an aluminum salt (called "fuller's earth"). Then he rubbed the paste on the dirty cloth. When it dried the salt crumbled, and the fuller removed the residue (including the soiling) with a wire-toothed comb or brush. He then rinsed the cloth in clear water. To bleach a white chiton he hung it up in a room filled with sulphur fumes. Sometimes he used human urine as a cleansing solution. Cleaning a *chiton* was an expensive process, and so the Greeks made great efforts to keep them unsoiled as long as possible.

Hair Styles and Cosmetics

In the days of Homer, Greek men wore their hair and beards long, but these were kept clipped and trimmed in the Golden Age. Not too short, however, because short-cropped hair was a sign of stinginess. (A miserly man had his hair cut close to his head so that it would take longer to grow in, so he'd have to pay for fewer haircuts.) The Spartans, of course, always wore their hair long as a sign of strength (and pulled it up to cushion their hard metal helmets).

Most Greek women had long hair, although the wealthiest women wore wigs. During the Golden Age it was stylish to wear one's hair up, tied with ribbons, scarves, or pieces of golden jewelry. The hair of slave women was clipped short.

A pale face was considered the most beautiful, and so powders made from white lead were often applied to a woman's skin to produce this effect. A pale complexion was a sign of nobility, since it contrasted strikingly with the deeply tanned faces of the peasant and slave women who labored in the hot

Ladies' hair fashions

sun. A Greek lady held a mirror of polished bronze attached to a slender handle when she applied her make-up or simply wished to admire herself. She used alkanet root to redden her cheeks and soot to line her eyes, and she anointed her body with sweet-smelling oils imported from Asia.

The Greeks loved jewelry, and the women wore many bracelets, necklaces, rings and drop earrings made of gold, silver, bronze, ivory, and bone. The jewelry of the wealthy was often adorned with precious stones such as lapis lazuli (a blue stone) and amber. Even the men enjoyed wearing metal rings, bracelets and headbands.

A Day in Athens

The average Athenian arose early, possibly awakened by the crowing of a rooster (a popular Persian import). He washed his face with the cool water in a pottery basin and cleaned his teeth by rubbing them with powdered pumice (volcanic ash).

Breakfast consisted of simple fare—bread, cheese, fresh fruit, such as pears, dates, or grapes, and perhaps a goblet of wine (which was always blended with water). Many Greeks were content to merely nibble on a lump of bread soaked in wine for breakfast. After his morning meal, a craftsman went to his workshop, probably a small room in the front of his house or one rented in another building. A more affluent citizen might spend a few hours studying the records of the crops produced on his country estates. Morning was also the time when government business was attended to.

Noon was market time, and the man of the house was responsible for the shopping. The marketplace was called the *agora*. It was the heart of the city. Surrounded by columned porches (called *stoa*) and government buildings, the *agora* was a bustling place where merchants exhibited their wares in wooden booths and haggled over prices with their customers. Woven

A well-dressed Greek woman

reed baskets displayed farm produce, such as olives, lettuce, onions, cheese, poultry, eggs, and grain as well as freshly caught fish from the local ports. The meat and fish were often placed on marble slabs, because the cool stone kept them fresher longer. Small shops selling lamps, cooking pots, and luxury goods occupied some of the buildings lining the *stoa*.

The marketplace attracted foreign traders as well as local ones. Merchants from Asia displayed beautifully woven cloth and jewelry, while traders from Cyprus offered copper tools and containers. Free men also went to the *agora* to hire workmen or to purchase slaves.

An Athenian citizen could easily spend an entire afternoon at the *agora*, not merely shopping but also strolling among the colonnades and gossiping with his friends. Actually, the original meaning of the word "agora" was "meeting," since from earliest times people would gather in the town center to discuss common issues.

As we have learned, the Greeks were introduced to the concept of coinage by Lydian traders in the Archaic Age. At first, every *polis* issued its own coins, but after the Persian Wars Athenian money became the standard currency throughout Greece. The two major units were the *obol* and the *drachma* (one *drachma* equaled six *obols*). The average Athenian earned about half a *drachma* (three *obols*) per day. No one in Greece carried a purse, and *chitons* had no pockets, so a merchant often put his coins in his cheek for safekeeping.

Apollo embodied the Greek ideal of a strong and healthy body as well as a well educated mind. The word *arete* means "excellence in everything", and it was the goal of every Greek citizen to be "well rounded." So an important part of an Athenian's day was a visit to the gymnasium, the ancient equivalent of a modern sports center, where he could work out to keep his body in prime condition.

The gymnasium was a large building with plenty of space to run, throw a discus or practice many of the other events performed in the Olympic Games. First, however, a man removed his clothing and handed it to his slave, who guarded it while his master was working out. (Remember those "chiton snatchers?") The word "gymnasium" comes from the Greek *gymnos* which means "naked." Greek athletes did not want their actions to be hindered by their loose-fitting garments. After undressing, the man entered the anointing room, where he covered his body with olive oil and then scraped it clean with a metal instrument called a strigil. This procedure removed dirt and sweat, and it was repeated after exercising.

A strenuous physical workout in the gymnasium was often followed by a refreshing bath. Afterwards, the man put on his *chiton* and strolled back to the *agora* to converse with his friends and neighbors in the cool shade of the *stoa*. What a pleasant way to spend the day!

An Athenian family enjoyed a cooked meal in the late evening after the heat of the sun had dissipated and refreshing breezes cooled the house. As we have learned, the head of the household reclined on a couch to dine. His wife served him and the children, and then she sat down on her straight-backed chair. Sometimes the family was served by their slaves.

Dinner was the main meal of the day, and it consisted of bread, fruit (figs and dates), nuts, vegetables (peas, lettuce, cabbage or lentils), cheese, and perhaps salted fish. The Greeks normally ate red meat only after animals were sacrificed at religious ceremonies. Cheese was made from goats' milk (cows' milk was considered fit only for calves). Onions and garlic garnished the fish and vegetables, and coriander and sesame were popular seasonings. Cakes saturated with honey made a delicious dessert. The

A light Greek supper

wine was diluted with water in large jugs called *kraters*. It was then poured into wide pottery goblets with two handles. The children drank goat's milk.

Honey cake: a tasty dessert

Banquets and Symposia

Frequently a man of comfortable means invited a few friends to his home for an all-male banquet. The number of guests would always range between three and nine (no less than the three Graces and no more than the nine Muses of mythology). The banquet took place in the men's quarters of the home (the *andron*). The host's wife directed the preparation and serving of the meal. Then she was obliged to remain in the *gynaeceum* until the banquet was over and it was time to clean up.

While family meals were fairly simple affairs, a banquet was often elaborate. Upon their arrival, the guests removed their sandals so that the household slaves could wash their feet. Then they took their places on the couches.

The main course of a banquet was usually fresh fish—some favorite dishes were fried shrimp, baked turbot with mulberry sauce, and bass steamed in brine with vegetables. Fowl such as thrush baked in honey or duck roasted with raisins were a special treat. The next course was nuts, fruit and cheese, followed by sweet cakes.

The food was served on pottery or metal plates which were placed upon low tables beside the dining couches. The men ate with their fingers. Metal spoons were sometimes used for liquid dishes, but usually a piece of bread made an efficient scoop (forks would not be invented for a thousand years.) A diner wiped his greasy hands on a piece of bread, which he then threw to the dogs.

Wine flowed abundantly at the banquets, although we must remember that it was diluted (its alcoholic content was considerably less than that of modern beer).

Lime, resin or seawater were frequently added to the wine to cut down on its acidity. Even today Greek wine often contains resin—this type of wine is called *retsina*. It was a time-honored tradition to spill a little wine on the floor at the beginning of a meal as an offering to the gods. This was an early form of saying grace.

A wine goblet

After the meal, the men discussed everything from local politics to the pettiest gossip. Of course, the wine continued to be poured, and so this part of the evening's entertainment was called the symposium, which means "drinking together". Sometimes symposia were held without a preceding banquet. (Today a symposium is a meeting of scholarly people to discuss particular subjects—without wine!)

During a Greek symposium the guests anointed their hair and beards with myrrh, and they placed wreaths upon their heads and around their necks. A toss of the dice selected a toastmaster for the evening. He proposed toasts and selected topics for discussion. He also set the proportions of water to wine. (Perhaps the amount of wine increased as the evening wore on.) Occasionally the men were entertained by musicians and dancing girls. A symposium could become a rowdy affair, since the Greeks did not frown upon becoming drunk. In fact, intoxication was considered a sign of wealth, since working men could not afford to deal with a hangover the next morning. The merry-making might last until the early hours of the morning, and the wife and slaves of the household would be busy all the next day putting everything back in order.

The people of the lower classes had neither the time nor the money to engage in such activities as banquets and symposia. In the evenings, they had a hearty meal of barley porridge sweetened with honey (or perhaps thick pea soup), cheese, onions, figs, and wine.

The Role of Greek Women

The life of a typical Greek woman was far less interesting than that of her husband, since she lived in a man's world. Most of her time was spent in the *gynaeceum* of her home. (Don't confuse *gynaeceum* with *gymnasium*). She hardly ever ventured out of her home, and then only when she was accompanied by another woman or a slave. If she attended the theater, she had to sit in the back row with the foreigners, and she could only see a tragedy since comedy was considered too bawdy for her delicate ears.

The duties of the wife of an Athenian citizen were to run the household, to spin wool and weave cloth for the family's clothing and blankets, and to raise the children. Greek women had no say in the government. They were not even allowed to own property or to conduct legal transactions. And so, from birth to death, a woman was under the control of a male relative, first her father, then her husband, and, if her husband died, her son. If she had no husband or son, her life was in the hands of her brother or her nearest male relative. The Athenian woman stood in sharp contrast to the typical Spartan woman, who was encouraged to interact with men, compete in athletic events, and to travel whenever she pleased.

A man could divorce his wife simply by making a statement of his intentions in front of witnesses. A woman, however, could do no such thing, since she had no legal rights. In the case of a divorce, the husband kept the

Statue of a pensive Greek woman

children and sent his former wife back to her family. He had to return her dowry, though.

Pericles once said that the ideal woman was the one who attracted the least attention. Even the great philosopher Aristotle defined woman as an imperfect form of man. For all their wisdom, the ancient Greeks had much to learn about equal rights.

An Athenian marriage was arranged by the fathers of the bride and groom. By the age of thirty a man was well established in business and able to afford a comfortable life style for his bride. He usually wed a young woman half his age so that she could serve him for many years. The family of the bride paid the groom a dowry (a gift of property or money).

Before her wedding, a girl placed her dolls upon the altar at a temple of Artemis. This act symbolized her coming of age—her putting aside of all childish ways. The bride wore bright clothing and a veil to her wedding. At the start of the ceremony an animal was sacrificed, and then its gall bladder was removed "lest bitterness mar the marriage." Often a bride saw her husband for the first time at the altar of marriage. After the solemn vows were taken, the guests threw grain and fruit at the couple, just as we throw rice today. This was their way of asking the gods to grant the couple many children. Afterwards, the husband carried his bride over the threshold of their new house, and they ate a special cake together.

Children

When a baby was born in Athens, the father had the right to accept or reject it. As in Sparta, a weak or frail child was rejected by the father and left on a lonely hillside to die from exposure. (The lucky ones were adopted by families, for whom they became slaves.) All too frequently in that male-dominated society, a baby was rejected simply because it was a girl.

A boy was usually named for his paternal grandfather. Greek names had special meanings. For example, Pericles means "very famous," Alcibiades means "son of a strong one," and Aristocles means "the best".

Hera, goddess of women and marriage

Athenian children up to the age of seven were raised by their mother and her slaves in the family home. If a child misbehaved, he might be threatened with a visit from Mormo (a monster who ate children) or Empusa (a hobgoblin who changed into many frightening shapes). In general, though, the lives of Greek children were care-free. They were doted upon by their parents as they played happily in the warm Mediterranean sunlight.

When Cleisthenes was in power he ordered all citizens to educate their sons. The girls stayed at home to learn domestic tasks. A special slave called a *pedagogue* taught his young master manners and escorted him to school. (Today "pedagogue" means "teacher.") At school the boy was taught to read, write, and to do math using an abacus. He held a metal stylus to practice writing upon a waxed tablet, and any mistakes he made were easily rubbed out. When the coating of wax became thin, a new layer was melted over it and the tablet was as good as new. Older boys wrote upon papyrus (a kind of paper made by the Egyptians) using pen and ink.

©PETER VAN DER SLUIS / WIKIMEDIA COMMONS

An original waxed tablet

The young students studied the great myths and legends of the past, and they often memorized hundreds of lines from Homer or Hesiod. They also learned to dance, sing, and play the flute or lyre. Indeed, a

Muse of poetry holds a lyre

well-educated Athenian gentleman was expected to be able to play the lyre and sing whenever called upon—"he who doesn't know how to play the lyre" was a proverbial description of an uneducated person. Of course, instruction in athletic events was an important part of a schoolboy's education, and he worked out at the gymnasium every day. A boy completed his education at the age of fifteen. Then he could become an apprentice to a craftsman or learn about his father's business.

At the age of eighteen a young man whose father owned property was eligible to become a citizen. A special ceremony was held in his honor at the temple of Zeus, where he was given the shield and spear of a warrior. He then swore an oath of citizenship, promising to be a good soldier, to preserve the Athenian constitution and to respect the Greek religion. A lock of his hair was cut and dedicated to the god of the heavens. Following the ceremony, a banquet was given in honor of the new citizen by his male relatives.

Upon becoming a citizen, an Athenian began his two years of military training. When he was twenty he signed up for active duty. He would be called up if Athens went to war. All free men in Athens had a military obligation. Soldiers had to supply their own equipment, and the richer the man, the better his armor and weapons. A wealthy man had a bronze (or iron) helmet, breastplate, and greaves as well as metal strips to protect his thighs. He might even ride a horse. A poor man had no armor except his shield. Many of the poorest men became rowers in the Athenian fleet.

Slaves and Metics

Slaves have been frequently mentioned in this chapter. It is probably surprising for you to learn that in the city acknowledged to be the birthplace of democracy nearly every family had slaves. The average household had three, but a wealthy man might have fifty. Even a family of modest means probably had at least one slave to do menial tasks. In 431 B.C.E. slaves made up about one third of the population of Attica.

Who were the slaves? They were usually the captives of war (or the children of captives), although some were purchased in the slave markets. Fortunately, the lives of the Greek slaves were not terribly hard. Those who were skilled often worked side by side with free Greek artisans and merchants.

Many slaves were paid a small amount for their labors, and this made it possible for some of them to eventually buy back their freedom. However, those slaves who were condemned to work in the silver mines of Attica led truly wretched lives. They were branded and chained together, and they often died of exhaustion.

Athenian democracy actually depended upon slavery. Were it not for the labor provided by the slaves, the Athenian citizens would not have been able to attend government meetings, serve on juries, or discuss political matters in the *agora*. This is one of history's great ironies.

Metics were foreign-born (non-Athenian) merchants, tradesmen and artists who made up a significant part of the middle class in Athens. There were about half as many *metics* as there were slaves. The *metics* were taxed, and they were expected to serve in the army. However, they could not own land, marry into a family of citizens, or vote. The *metics*, along with the slaves and the freedmen (former slaves), were the backbone of the Athenian economy.

Questions

1. Describe the basic layout of an Athenian house.
2. What was a gynaeceum?
3. How were the houses lighted at night?
4. What was a himation and how was it worn?
5. Describe the agora.
6. What were the major units of Athenian money?
7. What took place at the gymnasium?

8. What was the role of a typical Athenian woman?

9. What was a symposium?

10. Describe the education of the son of a Greek citizen.

Further Thoughts

1. When a boy was born in Athens, an olive wreath was hung on the door of his house to announce the good news to the neighbors. The birth of a girl was a less joyful occasion, for which a plain wooden circle or tuft of wool was placed on the door. Thus, from the very beginning of their lives females were treated as inferior human beings.

2. In Athens there were special officials to check weights and measures. They were called the *metronomoi*; ten men were chosen for the position each year. Another group of officials, the *agoranomoi*, checked the quality of products being sold in the agora. A third group was the money changers; they were called *trapezitai* "tablemen" because they worked at tables in the marketplace. They exchanged one kind of coins for another, charging a fee for each transaction, and they made so much profit that eventually they began to lend money out. This was the beginning of banking.

3. The Greeks loved horses. Ownership of one of those splendid beasts was the sign of an aristocrat. In fact, the Greek word horse (*hippos*) is included in many aristocratic names: the father of Pericles was named Xanthippos (meaning "tawny horse"), and the father of Alexander the Great (more about him later) was Philhippos ("horse lover"). When a Greek aristocrat died, his horse was always present at his funeral.

4. A son inherited his father's property, and if there was more than one, they would share it equally. If there was no son, a daughter could inherit, but she was required to marry the man chosen by her father, and he (the husband) became the actual heir.

5. Childbirth was a dangerous experience. There was no anesthesia to reduce pain and no medicine to prevent infection. Women were expected to have as many children as possible, since so many died at birth. Those women who survived the average of ten childbirths seldom lived beyond thirty-five or forty. Men on the other hand, could expect to live ten years longer than women.

Projects

1. The Greeks decorated their clothing and pottery with geometric designs, and many of these are copied by modern artists. In fact, the swastika is a Greek design found on many ancient vases. (The Greeks were but one ancient culture to use this design.) Below is a chart showing several designs and some Greek vases decorated with similar designs. Look in magazines and on the Internet for examples of Greek designs and use them to make a collage.

2. Make your own chiton. Take a large (king-sized) pillowcase. Cut a hole at one end for your head to slip through and two smaller holes near the top on the two sides for your arms. Decorate the bottom border of the garment with Greek geometric designs. Use a piece of cloth tied at the waist as a sash. A longer, roomier chiton can be fashioned from an old sheet following the same pattern. Wear the chiton for the performance of a Greek play or for a Greek party.

3. Cut up an old sheet or blanket (get permission first) into two pieces, and then sew them together to make one long piece of material. See if you can drape it like a Greek.

4. Have a Greek banquet. Everyone in the class can bring in a dish of typical Greek food (such as stuffed grape leaves, cucumbers in yogurt, or baklava). The specialties have not changed much over the centuries! Wear chitons and bring pillows to recline upon while dining. Be sure to have a lot of finger food, because forks are not allowed.

PART FOUR
THE LATER YEARS

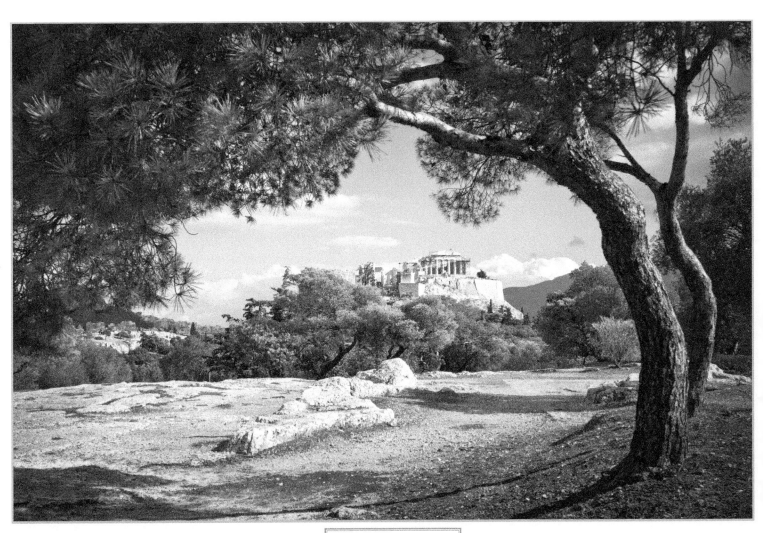

View of the Acropolis

CHAPTER 14

THE PELOPONNESIAN WAR

Despite the many cultural achievements of Athens during the Golden Age (or perhaps because of them), the members of the Delian League continued to grumble among themselves. They cherished their long tradition of independence, and the concept of a unified Greece seemed unnatural. Furthermore, the Athenians, who prided themselves on protecting the rights of individual citizens, were viewed by many of their kinsmen as bossy tyrants.

There were economic problems as well. Corinth, for example, had long enjoyed its status as a wealthy commercial center. But since the defeat of the Persians, the major trading port had shifted from Corinth to the Athenian port of Pireaus. The Corinthians saw their prosperity slowly dwindle.

Allied with Sparta
Allied with Athens

The two confederations

Forming Sides

The Spartans had never joined the Delian League. They depended upon their highly renowned military prowess to hold off any enemy attack, and since their city was located well inland, they had few worries about the Persian fleet. However, they did become increasingly concerned about Athens' expanding sphere of influence. We must remember that Sparta was run by military leaders who wished to maintain the status-quo at all costs. The idea of change made them cringe! So they worried about their territories being surrounded by democratic city-states controlled by Athens. Where would it all lead?

Sparta's displeasure was well-known throughout southern Greece, and when certain city-states of the Peloponnese decided they could no longer tolerate the overbearing Athenians, they naturally looked to the red-cloaked warriors for support. Eventually a series of minor skirmishes drew

A Spartan warrior

the Spartans into the conflict. The Spartan Alliance was formed, uniting the city-states of the Peloponnese, Corinth, and the region of Boeotia under the leadership of Sparta.

Mainland Greece was now divided into two confederations: the Delian League and the Spartan Alliance. It took only a minor incident involving a trading dispute to start the sparks flying, and in 431 B.C.E. war broke out. Called the Peloponnesian War by the Athenians, this unfortunate struggle of Greek versus Greek would last thirty years.

The major events of the war were carefully recorded and documented by a Greek historian named Thucydides in his book, *The Peloponnesian War*. Thucydides actually fought in the war (on the Athenian side) and took copious notes after each battle. He spoke with many of the military leaders in order to more fully understand their strategies, and he described these conversations in great detail in his book. He also interviewed eyewitnesses to the fighting and carefully examined the battle sites. Unlike Herodotus, Thucydides did not exaggerate figures or offer his personal views about events. Rather, he maintained a methodical and objective approach in describing historical events. So although

Herodotus is considered the Father of History, Thucydides was the first to impartially report on the major occurrences of his time.

A Ten-Year Stalemate

Pericles was in power in Athens when the war began. He recognized the superiority of the Spartan soldiers, and so he did all he could to avoid land battles, relying instead upon Athens' naval power. He was reassured by the two towering stone walls connecting the city with the seaport Piraeus, knowing that as long as the Athenian fleet ruled the seas, he could depend upon a steady supply of food from abroad. He hoped that eventually the Spartans would run out of supplies and leave Athens alone. (See map of the corridor on page 113.)

For ten long years small battles and skirmishes took place with neither side winning an advantage. Every summer, the Spartans ravaged the fields of Attica, destroying the grain, vineyards and olive groves with the aim of breaking the will of the Athenian people. During these trying times, the farmers and landowners sought refuge within the walls of the city.

Portrait of Pericles on a Greek coin

Meanwhile, the Athenian ships raided the coast of the Peloponnese, destroying whatever enemy ships they encountered. And so the war dragged on, no one able to break the impasse.

Pericles knew that he needed to encourage his people to endure the hardships caused by the war. He seized the occasion of a battle in which many Athenian soldiers had been slain to give a moving speech. After briefly praising the fallen soldiers, he proudly boasted of the great city for which they had given their lives. He described Athens as a shining light whose way of life would one day be copied by cities around the Greek world. (His entire speech appears in the Appendix.) As he had hoped, his words gave the Athenians the will to persevere in their struggle.

Athens Falters

The frequent sieges of the crowded city of Athens created uncomfortable and unsanitary living conditions, and the daily lives of the inhabitants steadily deteriorated. In 430 B.C.E., ships bearing grain from Egypt arrived at the port of Piraeus. They also carried a large number of rats, attracted to the grain. These rats were infected with a deadly disease causing an epidemic in northern Africa. Once the ships docked, many of the rats raced along the walled corridor to Athens. Fleas from the rats bit

and infected the Athenians, causing a terrible plague to break out. The high stone walls of the corridor confined the deadly disease to the city and spared the enemy soldiers stationed outside. Athens' lifeline had become an avenue of death.

Nearly a third of the population died, including Pericles himself. The passing of that highly respected leader marked a turning point in the Athenians' resistance to the Spartan advances. Matters grew steadily worse when Pericles was succeeded by men who lacked his judgment and authority.

The Persians played an important part in the Peloponnesian War. They well remembered their humiliating defeats at Salamis and Platea and the ensuing loss of the Ionian colonies. Over the years since then, Persian kings had sided with Sparta against the Delian League. During the Peloponnesian War the Persians supplied the Spartan Alliance with the resources to build up an impressive fleet of ships. They undoubtedly relished the thought of the Greek city-states going at each other, a process that would inevitably weaken them all. And they hoped that an Athenian defeat would restore to them their long lost territory in Ionia.

At the same time, the Persians understood the ways of the iron-handed Spartans whose government strongly resembled their own absolute monarchy. They were puzzled by the Athenian system that placed power in the hands of the ordinary people.

In spite of the aid the Persians gave to the Spartans, the war continued to drag on. In 421 B.C.E. both sides acknowledged their weariness with the whole thing and agreed to a temporary peace. The Greek people slowly returned to a more normal way of life, and all was well. But eight years later the peace was broken when the Athenians made an unwise decision: they attacked the city of Syracuse on the island of Sicily in order to obtain a new source of grain and cattle. They hoped that the conquest of Syracuse would make them the masters of the trade routes in the western Mediterranean.

The invasion was planned by a kinsman of Pericles named Alcibiades. He was a vain, selfish and impudent man who had gained power in the Athenian government through his guile and charm. The campaign was a military disaster from the beginning, and many Greek lives were lost. Those soldiers who survived the battles became the slaves of the Sicilians. They were condemned to labor in stone quarries for the rest of their

lives. The Greek fleet was partially destroyed, and although new ships were later built, the Athenian navy never recovered its former strength. Athens had lost her mastery of the seas, and Sparta gained an overwhelming advantage.

The End of the War

In 405 B.C.E. the Spartan navy, led by Lysander, surprised the Athenian fleet off the coast of Ionia and destroyed all its ships while the crews were inland enjoying a good

meal. The victorious Spartans now controlled the seas as well as the land. This was a fatal blow for Athens, because it severed the city's lifeline to the grain, timber and iron in the Greek colonies surrounding the Black Sea. When the Spartan ships blockaded Piraeus, the Athenians had no choice but to surrender.

Under the terms of the peace treaty, Athens gave up any surviving vessels and agreed to the destruction of all fortifications. The Athenian people watched in sorrow as the great walls that surrounded their city and extended to Piraeus were torn down by slaves working to the music of flutes. The Spartans rewarded the Persians for their support during the war by giving them the Ionian cities.

Although they were urged by some of their allies to kill the men of Athens, the Spartans refused to do so. They still remembered the heroism of the Athenian soldiers at the Battle of Marathon.

Sparta established a Council of Governors to rule Athens. This was led by a series of anti-democratic autocrats known as the Thirty Tyrants who made life miserable for nearly everyone until they were finally deposed after a year in 403 B.C.E. The democratic government was restored, and Athens became a center of learning. But the optimism and creativity that flourished after the Greek success in the Persian Wars was nearly snuffed out by the Athenian defeat by the Spartans. Scholars living in the aftermath of the war began to question whether it was possible to achieve happiness in an often hostile world. The Golden Age was gone.

The Defeat of Sparta

Sparta did not maintain military control over the rest of Greece indefinitely. In the fourth century B.C.E. a brilliant Theban general named Epaminondas devised a way to defeat the formidable Spartan soldiers. He knew that in a classic phalanx battle the winners were those soldiers who could push the hardest and break through the opposing line. So he restructured his formation so that the front line moved at an oblique angle, the left side considerably ahead of the right. He then strengthened the left flank by increasing the ranks from eight to fifty of his best fighting men. By the time the Theban center faced that of the enemy phalanx, its left flank had already broken through the right side of the enemy line. With the enemy's right flank thrown into disarray, the protruding Theban left flank could move inward to support the soldiers in the center. When the Theban soldiers on the right flank encountered the opposing phalanx, they were joined by the soldiers from the left and center sections. Now, the entire army crashed through what remained of the enemy line like a giant battering ram.

It was a simple strategy. The rapidly shifting front lines allowed the Theban soldiers to deliver a series of punches that were difficult for any army to withstand. The Spartans, trained for generations to march together in a straight line, were unprepared for such a change in tactics. Nor were they inclined to revise the traditional formation that had served them so well for so long.

Within a short period of time, the Thebans, with numbers far less than those of the Spartan troops, trounced the legendary red-cloaked warriors. At the Battle of Leuctra (371 B.C.E.) they proved themselves to be the best soldiers in Greece. After their victory, they freed the *helots* of Messenia. Sparta never recovered.

Questions

1. Why did many city-states resent Athens?
2. Why didn't the Spartans join the Delian League?
3. Who were the members of the Spartan Alliance?
4. What was Pericles' strategy?
5. How did the plague come to Athens?
6. What was the role of the Persians in the war?
7. What was Athens' fatal mistake?
8. What were the peace terms?
9. Describe Epaminondas' revolutionary battle plan.
10. Why was Thebes able to defeat Sparta?

The Battle of Leuctra

Further Thoughts

1. The funeral oration given by Pericles during the Peloponnesian War has frequently been compared with Lincoln's Gettysburg Address (see Appendix p. 181). Both leaders spoke of the heroism of the soldiers who had given their lives for their homeland and of the need for those still alive to carry on the battle. It is for the living, they said, to make sure that the ideals the soldiers have died for will not perish. Both speeches were delivered at a time when a people was feeling discouraged about a long drawn-out war. They sought to inspire the people to continue the struggle. Despite the fact that they were written many many years apart, they are amazingly similar in content and outlook.

2. Pindar was a poet living in Thebes who was famous for beautiful odes about the Olympic Games. He disapproved of Athens' determination to make every city-state a democracy, and he accurately predicted that the self-righteousness of the Athenians would bring about their own ruin. (As we learned earlier, the Greeks considered excessive pride, hubris, a major vice.)

3. Although he was a gifted military strategist, Alcibiades was perhaps the worst scoundrel in Greek history. He was a self-centered opportunist, completely lacking in scruples! Before leaving Athens to fight in Syracuse, he and some friends apparently went on a drunken rampage and defaced a group of stone statues of Hermes. When he was later summoned home to answer to the charges, he fled to Sparta. Once there, he told the Spartans how to attack an important town in Attica, and then he seduced the wife of one of the kings. For this he was condemned to death. Now he was a public enemy in both Athens and Sparta! But he used his charm to convince the Athenians to let him return, promising to get the Persians to help them against Sparta. He did manage to gain some Persian support (the Persians were always happy to play off one Greek city against another), and he later led an army against Sparta. Eventually his history of deceit caught up with him, and he found himself exiled once again from Athens. This time he sought refuge in Persia where, according to some accounts, he was later assassinated.

4. After the Peloponnesian War, many Greek soldiers became mercenaries (professional fighters for hire to other nations). A group of ten thousand Greek soldiers went to Babylonia (in modern Iraq) to fight for the Persian Prince, Cyrus. He was killed and they found themselves abandoned far from home, the targets of the troops of Cyrus' brother. The Persians killed the Greek leaders, and the soldiers marched northwest for 600 miles, fighting off enemy attacks, crossing mountains, and surviving extremely harsh weather conditions. They finally made it to the Black Sea, where they marched from city to city along the coast (these were Greek cities) until they finally reached their homeland. Known as the Ten Thousand, they became heroes of the Greeks. The march was described by the Greek historian Xenophon, who had participated in it.

5. Thucydides was intrigued by the contrasting cultures of Sparta and Athens. Here is a statement he made about them in his book: "If the city of the (Spartans) had been abandoned, and the temples and the foundations of the buildings remained, great, I think, would be the disbelief of its power

over such a long time from the past to the fame of the Spartans today. Athens, suffering from the same thing, would seem to have had twice the power it does, judging from the appearance of the city".

(translation by Daniel Arnaud)

Projects

1. Find out more about Athens' ill-fated attack upon Syracuse. Present a report about the battle to the class. Include a map showing the location of Syracuse.

2. Carefully study Pericles' funeral oration and Abraham Lincoln's Gettysburg Address in the Appendix. Then write an essay comparing and contrasting the two speeches. Be sure to describe the historical circumstances in which they were presented.

3. Lysistrata is a play by Aristophanes in which the women of Athens find a clever and practical solution to the Peloponnesian War. Find out what the solution was. Then write your own (short) version of the play, and perform it with several classmates.

4. Write a short play about the adventures and exploits of Alcibiades. Present it to the class.

5. "Persia was the real winner of the Peloponnesian War." What is the meaning of this statement? Do you agree or not? Write a short paper justifying your opinion.

CHAPTER 15

THE PHILOSOPHERS

The scholars who lived in Athens after the Peloponnesian War were very concerned about man's place in nature. They are known as philosophers. *Philosopher* is a Greek word that means "lover of wisdom." These early philosophers wanted to know more about how a society functioned. They pondered the meaning of happiness, and they wondered how this blissful state could be achieved. They questioned what was good and what was evil, and they wondered about the relation between an individual and the group. What were a person's moral responsibilities? What was virtue? Today, philosophy is the study of human conduct and the principles by which the members of a society can live together in harmony.

The three great philosophers of ancient Athens were Socrates, Plato and Aristotle. All brilliant men, they represented three generations of Athenians.

Socrates Asks Questions

Socrates lived from 470 until 399 B.C.E. As a young man he had fought in the Peloponnesian War. He once saved the life of Alcibiades in battle. Afterwards he served in the *Ecclesia.*

Socrates was greatly concerned about the effect the defeat by the Spartans had upon the spirit of the Athenian citizens. A huge number of young soldiers had been killed in that long, drawn-out war, commerce was at a standstill, and the vineyards, wheat fields, and olive groves of Attica had been virtually destroyed. It was a very difficult time for

everyone. Even after the Thirty Tyrants were booted out of power and a democratic government was restored, the new Athenian leaders lacked the confidence and optimism of Pericles. Athens was no longer the ruler of a great empire, and its leaders were groping for a new definition of their *polis.* They were uncertain and insecure, and because of this they nervously resisted any criticism of their policies. It seemed as though nearly everyone living in Athens was unhappy.

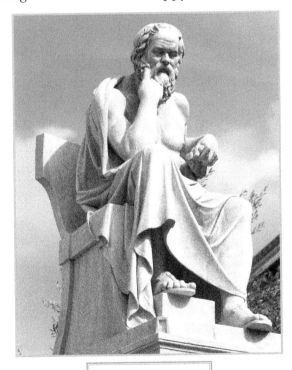

Statue of Socrates

Socrates wondered about this malaise, and he tried to figure out how the Athenians could recapture the old *joie de vivre* (love of life) of the Golden Age. He decided that the people were simply confused and overwhelmed by the destructiveness of recent events. Perhaps by turning away from the troubling past and looking deep within their own souls, they could create a more positive attitude. Socrates was convinced that knowledge of the world began with the understanding of one's self. He fervently proclaimed, "the unexamined life is not worth living."

He wandered about the agora, asking questions of everyone. "What is justice? What is wisdom? How do you define truth?" His most unsettling question was, "Do you really understand what you're talking about?" Socrates inquired of nearly anyone he met how men should behave, why something was good or beautiful when something else was not, and how a *polis* should best be governed. Whenever a question was answered, he immediately asked another. An encounter with Socrates must have been an exhausting experience, but before long he had quite a large following of intellectual young citizens who were intrigued with his refusal to accept anything at face value. He had become a teacher.

His systematic approach to learning was to start with a general topic and to slowly narrow it down to its essential parts until he got to the heart of the matter. By stripping away preconceived notions and unnecessary data like the peels of a banana, a person could arrive at the truth. This approach to learning is called deductive reasoning, and this way of teaching is known as the Socratic method.

Socrates believed that the gods had created the world for mankind, and therefore men should be god-fearing. But when he spoke of the gods, he referred to them as a single, all-powerful force. So he spoke of God rather than the gods, and this blasphemy (attack on the established religion) helped to bring about his ruin.

Arrest and Trial

The Athenian leaders felt extremely uncomfortable about Socrates' relentless questioning. Times had certainly changed. Pericles would have welcomed such a lively spirit of inquiry, but the officials of this era felt threatened by it. Furthermore, by emphasizing personal values Socrates seemed to suggest that the individual was more important than the state. This really angered the officials. And so when Socrates refused to stop his interminable questioning he was arrested. The government accused him of corrupting the young people by making them dismiss the role of the gods, and they called him a heretic (someone who opposes the official religion).

Socrates' death

Socrates had an opportunity to escape from his prison cell, but he refused to do so because he did not believe in breaking the law. At his trial he called himself "a gadfly" of the Athenian government. By this he meant that just as a fly bites a tired old horse and makes it jump, he questioned government policies in order to wake up the Athenians to the need for reform. He insisted that he was performing a helpful and necessary function for which they, his accusers, should be thankful.

Socrates probably could have saved himself, but he refused to admit to any wrong-doing. What was wrong with asking questions? The jury found him arrogant and annoying, and they sentenced him to death. He was seventy years old.

In those days a guilty citizen was forced to drink a poisonous brew made from hemlock. (The lower classes met more unpleasant ends.) Socrates was surrounded by his weeping friends and followers when the brew was brought to him. Before he drank it, he thanked the jailer who handed it to him, remarking that now he would have the good fortune to find out what death was like. He was curious to the end.

Enter Plato

Socrates never wrote anything down, but fortunately one of his pupils kept a detailed record of his words. This pupil was nick-named Plato, an epithet meaning "broad-shouldered" (his real name was Aristocles), and he lived from 427 until 347 B.C.E. Soon after the death of Socrates, Plato wrote an account of the trial and last moments of his master. Entitled *The Apology*, it glorifies the life and teachings of Socrates.

Plato also wrote a series of essays called *The Dialogues*. They resemble the script of a play in which people discuss issues of government and everyday living. They are based upon the conversations Socrates had with his followers in the agora. Plato's longest dialogue, *The Republic*, describes his vision of the ideal government. He did not support the democratic beliefs of Pericles—in fact, he felt that large groups of people often made bad decisions. Rather, he believed that society should be governed by an educated elite of philosophers. Included in this group were women, a notion not entertained by any of the other great thinkers of Greece. He was certainly ahead of his time.

Plato had a theory that all visible, tangible objects are unreal and that the things that we see are merely copies of ideas. For him, reality resided in the realm of ideas. Today such abstract reasoning about ideas

Statue of Plato

and reality is contained in a science known as metaphysics.

A poet and a scholar, Plato later opened a school for young citizens in an olive grove near Athens. Because this land was dedicated to the legendary hero, Academeus, the school was called the Academy. Teachers and students gathered there to discuss the intricacies of math and science as well as philosophy. Plato taught there for nearly fifty years. Today, an academy is a place of learning.

Aristotle's Thirst For Knowledge

The third of the great Greek philosophers was Aristotle (384-322 B.C.E.), a pupil of Plato. Aristotle also questioned the meaning of such concepts as truth and beauty, but his greatest interest was the natural world. He carefully examined the biological structure of living things. He arranged all the plants and animals he knew about into categories. He believed that everything had a special place in the universe.

Aristotle was also intrigued with human political structures, and in *The Politics* he wrote that men should use their logic rather than their emotions to govern themselves (remember Euripides?). He agreed with Plato that people of education and talent should rule the *polis*. He justified slavery by arguing that non-Greeks were inferior beings who ought to serve their betters, the Greeks (*Hubris*, again!). His interest in literature is reflected in *The Poetics*, which includes a thoughtful and comprehensive analysis of drama and how it reflects Greek society.

Like his mentor Plato, Aristotle set up his own school in Athens. Called the Lyceum, it was a pleasant place where the

Statue of Aristotle

teachers walked around the *peripatoi* (a columned porch in the garden), sharing their knowledge and wisdom with their students much as Socrates had once done. For this reason, Aristotle and his followers were known as the "peripatetics." Today a peripatetic is a person who is always on the move.

Aristotle was the first Greek scientist to follow a systematic method of inquiry and observation, and he wrote many books about his discoveries. He became so famous that King Philip of Macedonia asked him to teach his thirteen-year-old son, Alexander. We will learn more of this relationship in the next chapter.

Questions

1. What does the word "philosopher" mean?

2. Why were the Athenians unhappy?

3. What was the most important thing in life, according to Socrates?

4. Why was Socrates condemned by the government officials?

5. What was the Academy?

6. How did Plato feel about the democratic ideas of Pericles?

7. Who made the best governors, according to Plato?

8. What was Aristotle's greatest interest?

9. What does the word "peripatetic" mean?

10. Who was Aristotle's most famous pupil?

Further Thoughts

1. Today teachers often use the Socratic method in the classroom. Like Socrates, they encourage students to ask questions about what they are learning rather than to simply accept what is written in a book. Do you find that group discussions (with thought-provoking questions tossed about) help you to understand what you are studying?

2. A student of Socrates once visited the Oracle of Delphi. The oracle proclaimed that the philosopher was wise, and at his trial Socrates referred to this description of himself. He then added that he must be the wisest of all men since he alone knew that he knew nothing.

3. The Stoics were a group of philosophers led by Xenon. They got their name from the stoa (the porch of the agora) where they met. They believed that nature was controlled by the gods and that if a person simply acted naturally, he could be happy. The Stoics believed in living calmly and reasonably. Since all men were brothers, they should live together in harmony. The important thing was not to achieve a goal or to change the world, but rather to lead a virtuous life. Today, a stoic is someone who accepts his fate without complaining.

4. Socrates had a brilliant mind, but he did not possess the handsome body portrayed in classical Greek statues. He had a waddling gait, a snub nose, bulging eyes, and a pot belly! Nor was his domestic life ideal. He had a shrewish wife named Xanthippe, and once when he was teased about her nagging behavior he replied, "My great aim in life is to get on well with people. I chose her (Xanthippe) because I knew if I could get on with her I could with anyone!"

Projects

1. Protagoras was a Sophist (a kind of philosopher) who said that "man is the measure of all things." Find out who the Sophists were and then explain the meaning of this famous statement. How did it challenge the traditional Greek religious beliefs?

2. Diogenes was a philosopher with some unusual ideas. He went barefoot, wore rags, let his hair grow long and walked around with a lantern in the daylight looking for an honest man. He snarled at what others considered proper behavior. Some said that his search for integrity forced him to live like a dog. The Greek word for doglike is cynic. Find out who the Cynics were and what they believed. (Today a cynic is someone whose ideas go against public opinion.)

3. Some philosophers believed that man should spend his time pursuing pleasure (hedone). Write a short report about the Hedonists.

4. Epicurus proposed a "comfortable" philosophy. Learn more about it, and

compare this approach to life with that of the Stoics.

5. Plato made up an imaginary island for the setting of one of his dialogues. He called it Atlantis. Ever since, people have been trying to find this mysterious island, which supposedly sank into the sea. Was it real or purely fictional? Find out more about Atlantis and present a short report about it to the class.

6. Write a dialogue in which Pericles and Plato argue about what is the best form of government.

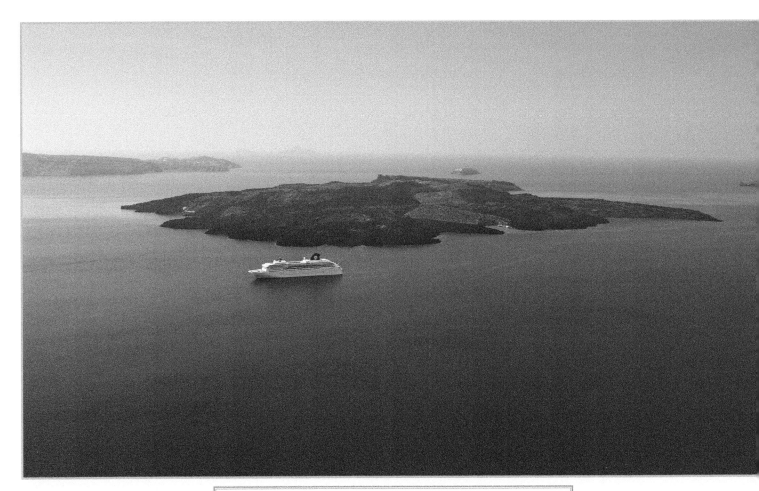

Some say Plato modeled Atlantis on the island of Santorini

CHAPTER 16

ALEXANDER THE GREAT

As the Greek city-states continued to bicker with one another after the Peloponnesian War, a new power was growing stronger day by day to the north. This was the kingdom of Macedonia, a land of backward, hard-living warriors who, although they spoke a dialect of Greek, were considered barbarians by the more civilized peoples of the long established city-states. The Macedonians had no love for the Greeks, and they had supported the Persian invaders in the previous century.

Philip Builds Up His Army

In 359 B.C.E. Philip II inherited the throne of Macedonia. As a boy, Philip had

Sarissas

Macedonia and Greece, including colonies under Persian Control

spent time in Thebes as a captive of war. He had carefully studied the phalanxes when they were drilling, and he marveled at the clever tactics of Epaminondas. Now that he was in power, he set out to improve upon the formation and strategies of the Theban army in order to make his own forces invincible.

Philip invented a very long (eighteen-foot) spear called the *sarissa*, which was carried by the soldiers in the rear ranks of his phalanx. When these heavy spears were held upright, they hid maneuvers occurring behind the phalanx. When they were lowered for an attack, they were grabbed and held by the men in the front ranks. The spears protruded through the front line of the phalanx like the quills of a giant porcupine, bristling from flank to flank. This must have been a frightening sight for any enemy.

Philip added a swift moving cavalry to his infantry. There were few horses in the mountainous lower Greek peninsula, but the gently rolling hills of Macedonia provided excellent pasture-land. Sturdy, spirited horses were raised in great numbers there, and Macedonian boys became excellent horsemen at an early age. Philip's cavalry corps was made up of young aristocrats known as the Companions. They made the phalanx even more effective by protecting its flanks and rear. Under Philip's leadership the Macedonian cavalry became the most renowned horsemen in the ancient Mediterranean world.

Patriotism played an important role in the new army. At a time when the Greek city-states depended more and more upon mercenary (hired foreign) soldiers because the local citizens no longer felt the old loyalty to their homeland, Philip built up a well-disciplined, extremely loyal organization of warriors.

Philip respected the rich culture that had flourished in Athens during the Golden Age, and he longed to unify all of Greece with his own kingdom. He knew that his timing was right—city-states were so busy squabbling with each other that they took no notice of his steady build-up of troops. Whenever he could, Philip encouraged dissension among the Greek states to further divert attention from his military plans. Then he struck. He invaded the Greek cities that lay between Macedonia and the coast of the Aegean so that he could gain access to the port cities.

Philip Conquers Greece

Now that he had a toehold in Greece, he was ready to begin his attack upon the major cities. Too late, the Greek armies recognized the strength of the Macedonian forces as Philip swept down and subdued them one by one. At Chaeronea he handily defeated the Athenian troops, and this victory ended the Greek resistance, at least for the time being.

Philip then organized the Greek city-states into the "Hellenic League." He referred to himself as "protector" of the league, for he was keenly aware of the Greeks' disdain for kings. He wanted to win the respect and support of the people he had conquered, not fuel their anger. Each *polis* was allowed to retain its own local government, but the Greeks had to promise not to fight among themselves anymore or to try to overthrow him. To no one's surprise, Sparta refused to join the league.

Philip had his eyes on more than the Greek mainland. His plan was to incorporate Greek soldiers into his Macedonian army and then march his expanded forces eastward to battle the Persians. His goal was to win back the Ionian cities that had been in Persian hands since the end of the Peloponnesian War. Under his guidance and military might, the old Athenian empire could well be restored, but this time it would be controlled by Macedonia.

The Young Alexander

Philip had several wives. His first wife, Olympias, bore him a son named Alexander. Since Philip was anxious to bring Athenian culture to Macedonia, it was logical for him to choose the learned philosopher Aristotle

Bust of young Alexander

to tutor his young son. (Aristotle, in fact, had grown up in Macedonia.) Alexander was a bright and imaginative student, and he was enraptured by Aristotle's reading of *The Iliad*. He never tired of hearing the exciting stories about the times of Agamemnon and Menelaus. Achilles became his hero. He dreamed of one day becoming as brave a warrior as that gallant Greek champion who had slain Hector at Troy. Throughout the rest of his life, Alexander always slept with a copy of *The Iliad* under his pillow.

Aristotle instilled in his student an appreciation for the natural environment, and he encouraged him to be open to new ideas and unfamiliar situations. This lesson would serve Alexander well on the battlefield, as we shall see. Thanks to the efforts of his father and his tutor, the young prince came to love Greek art and poetry, convinced that Athenian culture represented the height of all human endeavor.

As Alexander grew older, he proved himself an excellent horseman. There is a famous story about how he tamed the black stallion that he was to ride for most of his life. According to the legend, a horse trader once brought a very high-spirited stallion to sell to Philip. No one could handle the horse, who reared and bolted whenever someone tried to mount him. The prince watched attentively, and then he asked his father if he might have a try. Philip could not imagine his son succeeding where grown men had failed, but he admired his spirit and so he agreed to the request. Alexander (following the advice of Aristotle to observe everything closely) had noticed that the horse jumped back whenever he saw his own shadow. So he grabbed the reins and led the horse toward the sun; then he scrambled aboard and galloped off in the same direction. Since there was no shadow, the horse showed no fear and was easily controlled. Once he had mastered the animal, Alexander was able to guide him back to where his father stood. Philip cried tears of joy when he saw his son's accomplishment, and he exclaimed, "Alexander, you must find another kingdom

A spirited stallion much like Bucephalus

to rule, for Macedonia is surely too small for you!" Truer words were never spoken.

Philip gave his son the horse, which was named Bucephalus (meaning "bull head"). No one could ever control the stallion except Alexander, for whom he became as docile as a lamb. Bucephalus would even lower his great head so that his young master could more easily mount him.

Alexander was made a member of Philip's cavalry when he turned sixteen. Even at this early age, the prince won the respect of the Macedonian horsemen by his skill and boldness in battle. When Philip's army invaded Greece, Alexander (and Bucephalus) led one wing of the cavalry, while his father commanded the other. Together they led the Macedonian army to victory after victory.

Alexander Becomes King

Philip's dream to win back the Ionian cities from the Persians was not to be. While attending the wedding of his daughter in 336 B.C.E., he was stabbed in the back. No one knows who planned the murder. Most scholars suspect that his jealous first wife Olympias was behind the plot. Others suspect the Persians. Some even suspect Alexander. But regardless of who was responsible for Philip's death, his son suddenly found himself ruler of Macedonia and Greece at the age of twenty.

The Greeks were relieved to hear of Philip's death, and they assumed that Alexander could quickly be driven out of their homeland. The boy didn't seem much of a threat. He was only five feet six inches tall, and his clean shaven face and flowing blond hair underscored his youth. But Alexander was supremely confident in his ability to command. He had inherited his father's ambition and organizational genius, and he was willing to take risks to achieve his goals. Furthermore, he was loyally supported by the Macedonian army.

Alexander moved swiftly. He imprisoned the Greek leaders who were plotting against him, and he claimed Philip's title for himself. Then he marched north to put down a revolt by tribesmen in Illyria, a rugged territory controlled by Macedonia. When a rumor circulated in Greece that Alexander had been killed in battle, the city-states, led by Thebes, organized a rebellion against the troops Philip had installed there. Alexander raced to Greece with his men and defeated the rebellious armies. Philip's long *sarissa* spears and the aggressive cavalry charge of the Companions overwhelmed even the long-invincible Theban phalanxes.

Alexander decided to make Thebes an example of what might happen to any Greek *polis* that resisted him. He destroyed the city, sparing only the house of the poet Pindar, whose verses he had studied with Aristotle and greatly admired. Twenty thousand Thebans who survived the assault were sent into slavery.

On to Asia

Once he had regained control of Greece and those Macedonian provinces that had rebelled, Alexander set out to accomplish his father's goal—the liberation of the Ionian cities. He crossed the Hellespont, just as Xerxes had done over a century before, leading nearly 40,000 Macedonian and Greek soldiers. (Only Sparta did not contribute troops to his army.) He would never return to Europe.

Greece, the Hellespont and Asia Minor

While the ships bearing his troops landed on the Asian coast, Alexander sailed south. Ever the romantic, he had the burning desire to retrace Agamemnon's path to Troy. Once ashore, he set out for the ancient walled city, dramatically quoting passages of *The Iliad* to his comrades as he marched. (Thanks to Aristotle, he had memorized the entire epic.)

When he arrived at Troy, Alexander placed a wreath upon the grave of Achilles and made a sacrifice at the temple of Athena. Bowing his head at the altar, he vowed to end the struggle between Europe and Asia that had begun so many years before when (according to Homer) Paris abducted Helen. He removed an ancient shield from the temple which he would later carry into battle for good luck.

Alexander then rejoined his men, and they soon came face to face with the enemy at the Granicus River. The local Persian satrap had placed a line of cavalry along the far shore of the river backed up by a phalanx of mercenaries.

Alexander carefully studied the enemy formation. Then he ordered his men into position (the foot soldiers flanked by the cavalry). Suddenly he charged, leading the Companions at a full gallop across the river and up the steep bank on the other side. He moved with such speed and decisiveness that the Persian horsemen were caught off guard. The Companions easily smashed through the enemy line and began hand to hand combat. Alexander was nearly finished off by a Persian cavalryman who attacked him from behind, but his boyhood friend, a dark-bearded man named Cleitus, saved his life by literally slicing off the Persian's arm—sword and all.

The Macedonian foot soldiers then waded across the shallow river and pushed the enemy into retreat with their solid line of spears. It was a glorious day for Alexander. After the battle, he sent 300 sets of captured Persian armor to the Athenians as tokens of his victory, along with the message that he owed his success to the Greek allies "except the Spartans" (the red-cloaked warriors who had refused to join his campaign).

From the Granicus, Alexander marched southwest to free the Ionian cities, fulfilling his father's dream. He then moved northeast to Gordium, the capital of the ancient kingdom of Phrygia. According to yet another legend, the yoke of the chariot of a former king named Gordias was tied by an intricately knotted rope (known as the Gordian knot) to a post outside a temple of Zeus. Everyone in the kingdom knew the prophecy connected with the knot: the man who could untie it would conquer all of Asia. For Alexander the temptation must have been irresistible. He cautiously approached the yoke and studied the knot. Then, deciding that he could not untie it, he quickly drew his sword and sliced through it. In his mind he had succeeded in the task, for had he not disposed of the knot and freed the yoke from the post?

Cutting the Gordian knot

This episode vividly illustrates the way Alexander typically dealt with a challenge: after carefully examining the principle aspects of the problem, he would spring to action and decisively resolve it. And, as we shall see, the prophecy of the Gordian

Knot would indeed be fulfilled. Today, "to untie the Gordian Knot" means to solve a difficult problem quickly and decisively.

Clashes with Darius III

As Alexander moved south from Gordium, a huge Persian army assembled. The king of Persia at this time was Darius III. He had come to power the very same year as Alexander. As we know, the Persians always referred to their monarch as the Great King, and Darius certainly lived up to the image, at least physically. He was a very tall man for those early times (at a towering six feet six inches he was a foot taller than Alexander),

Black Sea

Granicus

Gordium

Saridis

Ephesus

Issus

Mediterranean Sea

Tyre

Alexandria

Memphis

Temple of Amon

Alexander's route to Egypt

and his full black beard made him appear virile and all-powerful. Darius was a proud and haughty man. There was some cause for his arrogance: he ruled an empire covering two million square miles!

The Persian force was massive. One part of it was made up of Greek soldiers, who served as mercenaries. Their numbers were equal to those of Alexander's entire army. The Persian forces slowly advanced to meet the Greeks at Issus, Syria. But Alexander wasn't too worried. He figured that its vast size and lack of discipline would make the enemy army unwieldy. He had also heard stories about the indecisive (some said cowardly) personality of Darius.

Issus was a narrow plain between the sea and the mountains, and its restricted space prevented Darius from using all of his troops. When he scanned the ranks of enemy soldiers facing him, Alexander looked for a weakness. Suddenly, he saw a gap in the front line. Wasting no time, he charged at a full gallop, leading his lightning-fast Companions through the gap, followed by the tightly-knit phalanx of soldiers wielding their long metal-tipped *sarissas*. When Darius caught a glimpse of Alexander guiding Buchephalus toward him, a gleaming sword raised above his head, he panicked and fled the battle in his golden chariot. This unexpected desertion by the king left his army in utter confusion, and thousands of Persian troops were trampled by their fellow soldiers.

Darius also abandoned his mother, wife and daughters, who were waiting in a camp nearby. Alexander made the women his prisoners, but he treated them with chivalry and respect. He was disgusted that "the Great King" had deserted his family, and

he couldn't imagine why he had brought them so dangerously near the field of battle in the first place. When Alexander entered Darius' abandoned tent, he was dazzled by the priceless jewels, gold and silver tableware, inlaid furniture, golden throne and elaborate bath tub set up there. As he sat down to the feast that had been prepared for the Persian monarch, he exclaimed, "So this is what it is like to be king!" It was his first encounter with the luxuries of the East.

Meanwhile, Darius was anxious for peace at any price, and so he sent ambassadors to Alexander offering a rich ransom as well as most of Anatolia. Alexander refused the offer, adding that he would not be paid off with land that he already owned. When Parmenio, one of his generals, suggested, "I would accept this if I were Alexander," the young king disdainfully replied, "and so would I, if I were Parmenio!"

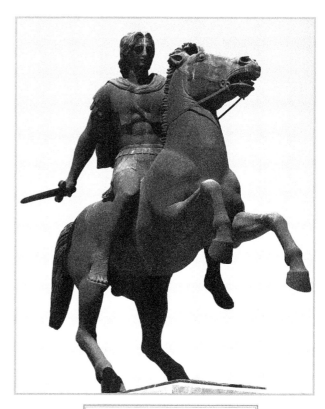

Alexander and Bucephalus

Alexander Gains Control of the Coast

After the stunning victory at Issus, the Greek army swept south along the Mediterranean coast of Asia. Alexander worried that Darius might receive support from his fleet of ships, and so he decided to cut off communications between the Persian sea and land forces. With this goal in mind, he conquered the territories of Phoenicia and Palestine. Then he moved south to besiege the island port city of Tyre, a Phoenician city controlled by Persia. The siege lasted for seven months, but Alexander finally triumphed by building a bridge of stone and cedar beams across the mile-wide channel separating Tyre from the mainland. Across this bridge his men dragged catapults and siege towers for a final assault of the island fortress. With this victory, Alexander could claim control of the entire eastern Mediterranean coast.

Sojourn In Egypt

In 332 B.C.E. Alexander entered Egypt. This rich civilization that had flourished for nearly 3,000 years had been conquered by the Persians in the sixth century B.C.E. The Egyptian people hated their foreign masters, and they joyously welcomed Alexander as their liberator and the rightful ruler of their nation. Alexander always respected foreign customs, and he knew that religion lay at the heart of Egyptian culture. Therefore, soon after his arrival in Egypt he set out for the ancient city of Memphis to offer sacrifices to the Egyptian gods.

The young conqueror had so enjoyed learning about the natural world with Aristotle that he brought several scientists along with him on his long journey. He frequently sent specimens of plant life back to his former teacher, who now lived in Athens. While in Egypt, Alexander dispatched a party of men to Nubia (modern Sudan) to discover the cause of the annual flooding of the Nile. They reported that the heavy spring rains in the mountains to the southeast combined with the melting snow caused the river to flood its banks. Until then, the Egyptians believed the yearly inundation was an act of the gods.

A Persian cavalryman

As Alexander walked about the ancient tombs and temples that line the Nile, he might have been reexamining his reasons for leading an army across two continents. His ambitions had certainly grown since he first crossed the Hellespont. He now controlled not only Ionia but Egypt and the western coast of Asia as well. It was clear that his military capabilities were extraordinary— what new conquests could they lead to? Alexander was fascinated by the Asian and African cultures he had encountered, and perhaps he pondered ruling an empire made up of a diversity of peoples. Or maybe he simply craved power.

The expanding empire needed a centrally located city to coordinate trade in the eastern Mediterranean. The coast of Egypt seemed the ideal location, and Alexander selected a site in the Nile delta overlooking a protected harbor. Kneeling on the sand, he drew with a reed his plan for the city: the streets were to be arranged in a grid, and there would be temples, government buildings, markets and places for scholars to gather and study. Of course, the city would be named Alexandria (many Alexandrias were to be founded throughout the young king's travels, but this one was destined for greatness). Alexander appointed an architect named Dinocrates to oversee the construction of the city, but he would not live to see its completion.

From there he crossed the scorching sands of the western desert to visit the oasis of Siwa, the site of the holy shrine of the god Amon. The priests of Amon's temple acknowledged Alexander as the legitimate Pharaoh (king of Egypt); since the Egyptians considered their Pharaoh a living god, Alexander now held a divine status. He must have enjoyed this new role. Coins made soon after this time show him wearing ram horns, the symbol of Amon.

A coin showing Alexander with a ram's horns

Back to Persia

Alexander remained in Egypt for six months. But he knew that Darius was waiting for him, and so he returned to Asia, leading his troops across the Euphrates River to the banks of the Tigris in Mesopotamia (modern Iraq) for a final showdown.

At Gaugamela the Persian king had assembled an army even larger than the one he led at Issus (his troops now outnumbered Alexander's five to one), and he had a secret device—50 war chariots with deadly scythe blades attached to their wheels. The Great King planned to use these gruesome vehicles to literally cut through the Macedonian phalanx.

Alexander spent the night before the battle carefully studying the layout of the field and planning his strategy. The next day he placed lightly-armed foot soldiers in front of his phalanx. When the chariots charged, these agile men jumped aside to avoid the blades and then hurled their javelins at the charioteers. Then the phalanx split in two, allowing the horses to draw the empty chariots through the gap. Once that obstacle had been dealt with, Alexander led the Companions and the infantry in a swift attack against the Persian line. Remembering Darius's cowardly nature, he galloped directly toward the Great King; as expected, Darius turned tail and fled. When the Persian soldiers realized that they had once again been deserted by their leader, they lost heart and retreated. Darius was later assassinated by his own bodyguard.

The victorious Macedonians marched from Gaugamela to the ancient city of Babylon, where the people quickly surrendered without any bloodshed. Alexander honored the local gods and ordered the restoration of the sacred Babylonian shrines that had been damaged by the Persians. Then he continued on to Susa, where he helped himself to the sacks full of gold coins lying in Darius's royal vaults. He sent many of the coins back to the Greek city-state of Platea, because its soldiers had fought so bravely during the Persian War.

It was winter, but in spite of the bad weather, Alexander led his men over the mountains to Persepolis, the capital of the Persian empire and the site of its rich central treasury (worth half a billion dollars!). The local soldiers hadn't expected an invasion at that time of the year, and so he met little resistance. Alexander later assembled caravans using 20,000 mules and 5,000 camels to carry the golden treasure back to Greece.

By now his men desperately needed a rest, and so Alexander spent the remainder of the winter in Persepolis. But after many weeks of luxurious living, this pleasant interlude came to an abrupt end when Darius's beautiful palace in which Alexander

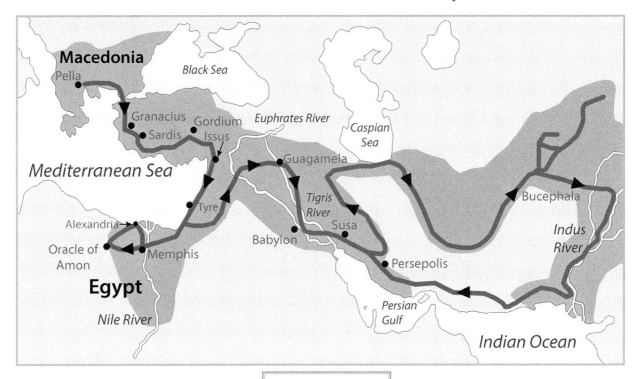

Alexander's march

was living burned to the ground. Alexander was unhurt. No one is certain why the palace was destroyed, but some scholars believe that Alexander ordered its destruction in revenge for Xerxes' burning of Athens over a century earlier. Others suggest that he was drinking heavily with his generals and that he (or someone else) simply started the fire "for kicks."

After the fire, Alexander's thoughts turned back to his empire. He was now master of Persia and incredibly rich. He could have returned to Macedonia. Instead, he marched east to consolidate the distant regions of what had become his empire. He battled many tribal warriors, but they were no match for his army. It seemed to everyone that Alexander was invincible, and in military matters he certainly was: in his lifetime he never lost a single battle.

A New Demeanor

As Alexander piled up victory after victory, his men noticed a change in his attitude and demeanor; some worried that he was turning into a Persian. Indeed, the new Great King began to wear the purple robes of Persian royalty, and he even married an Asian princess, Roxanne (some say she was his one true love). And his decision to hire Persian mercenaries was viewed by his men as a tremendous insult. They thought it was wrong to dilute their ranks with foreigners (especially former enemies). But a greater blow was yet to come. Intrigued by the court etiquette of the Asians, Alexander decided to adopt many local royal customs. Most offensive to his men was his insistence that they kneel before him. The Greeks had never treated their leaders in such an idolatrous manner (nor even their gods, for that matter), and they refused to do so now. Alexander did not press the issue and later abandoned the idea, but the old feeling of comradery and mutual support that he had shared with his men in the early days was disappearing.

The growing uneasiness erupted into violence one night when Alexander was drinking heavily with his generals. Cleitus, the soldier who had saved Alexander's life at Granicus, proposed a toast to Philip, crediting him with the Greek victories in Asia because he had created the Macedonian army in the first place. Alexander, angered by not receiving full credit for his successes, seized a spear and fatally stabbed his old friend. He later regretted what he had done, but his men never forgave him.

Perhaps in an effort to cast off his feelings of guilt, Alexander ordered his men to prepare for yet another march. This time they headed northeast across a rugged terrain until they reached a river in Russia that supposedly marked the end of the world; another city (Alexandria the Farthest) was founded there. As he had done every time he conquered or established a city, Alexander left behind a number of his men to serve as governors and to introduce the ideals and principles of Greek culture to the local people. Then he headed south.

On to India

In 327 B.C.E. Alexander's army crossed the western part of the towering Himalayan Mountains (the Hindu Kush). The scientists in his party charted the areas they crossed, and their maps were to be of great value

Silhouette of a war elephant

to later Europeans' understanding of the geography of Asia.

In those days the Greeks believed that India was a small peninsula whose eastern shores were washed by a vast body of water called Ocean. For this reason, Alexander was convinced that once he reached the eastern coast of India his empire would extend to the end of the earth. It was an exciting possibility.

On the far side of the Hindu Kush stretched the wide plain of the Punjab. The Indus River cuts through the plain on its way to the Indian Ocean. It was here that Alexander faced his most difficult battle. An army that included 200 war elephants was waiting for him on the far shore of the river. Its leader, a local monarch named Porus, was mounted on one of the largest elephants. Porus himself was a tall man (some say he was seven feet tall) and he was a shrewd and courageous adversary.

Alexander devised a strategy for dealing with the elephants. He ordered his light infantry to throw their spears at the drivers riding atop the huge beasts and to prod the animals with their daggers. The plan worked fairly well, and many of the elephants panicked and trampled the Indian foot-soldiers. But Porus' men fought on with such determination and skill that the battle lasted for hours.

When the fighting was over Alexander had won—but it was to be his last great battle. King Porus was taken prisoner, and when Alexander asked him how he expected to be treated, the proud monarch responded, "Like a king!" Alexander was always impressed by men who showed personal courage and dignity, and so he restored to Porus his kingdom, with the understanding that it would be ruled as a part of his own empire.

Alexander's last battle coincided with the death of his faithful steed Bucephalus. The gallant black stallion that had carried his master thousands of miles finally died of the accumulated effects of his war wounds and old age. Alexander was greatly saddened by the loss of Bucephalus, and he buried him with great pomp and ceremony. He founded a city (Bucephala) at the site of the stallion's grave.

Turning Back

Alexander continued marching eastward, determined to reach the waters of Ocean. But his men were exhausted, and they were dispirited by rumors that there was yet another great river (the Ganges) to cross before they reached India's eastern shoreline. Many of them had followed their king faithfully for nearly 3,000 miles, but now they refused to take another step. They begged him to return home.

Alexander moped in his tent for three days (just as Achilles had done in *The Iliad*), and then he finally acknowledged that he had no choice but to turn back. He insisted, however, that he return by a different route than he had come. To do otherwise would imply a retreat. Besides, he was eager to explore new territories and perhaps conquer more land.

He divided his forces, sending one group by boat to the mouth of the Indus River from whence it would proceed westward along the coast to the Persian Gulf. Two other groups marched by land, one of them led by Alexander. His return trip was the most difficult part of the entire journey. After reaching the mouth of the river and following the southern coast of India, he came to some mountains and was forced to march inland through a scorching desert. Supplies quickly ran out, and the starving troops had to slaughter the baggage animals in order to survive. Nor was it easy to find the way. The staggering soldiers frequently got lost in the blowing desert sands. They marched at night to avoid the blistering heat of the sun, but they did not always escape the hazards of flash floods, poisonous snakes or hostile tribesmen.

As ever, Alexander shared the hardships of his men. He sent his own horse to the rear and marched on foot with his troops, refusing water when there was not enough for everyone. The trek homeward was a nightmare. During the sixty-day march thousands of his men died of thirst, starvation, and heat stroke.

When they finally arrived in Susa, the surviving soldiers eagerly consumed large quantities of water and then collapsed from utter exhaustion. When he and his men recovered their strength, Alexander moved on to Babylon, where he punished the corrupt local officials who had taken advantage of his absence and then reorganized the city government.

Alexander had now begun to seriously think of himself as a Greco-Persian, and he probably dreamed of ruling a multinational empire founded upon the Greek way of life. To symbolize the mingling of Greek and Persian cultures, he ordered his soldiers to marry Asian women in a mass ceremony; he himself married two of the daughters of Darius. Soon afterwards, Alexander arranged for 30,000 Persian youths to begin military training under Macedonian instructors.

Most of Alexander's men did not share his vision of a Greco-Persian society, and they continued to complain about diluting their ranks with foreign blood. More and more they questioned their leader's sanity. There seemed good cause for this when Alexander announced that he should henceforth be recognized as the son of Zeus-Amon (a deity having the attributes of the Greek god Zeus and the Egyptian god Amon). Did he actually believe the words of the priests at Siwa? When news of his proclaimed deification were sent to Greece, the Spartans replied with characteristic understatement, "Let Alexander be a god if he wants to." They were not impressed.

The Death of Alexander

Alexander soon grew restless in Babylon, and he began to make plans to conquer Arabia. But this campaign never took place. In June, 323 B.C.E. he fell ill with a high fever. No one is sure whether he contracted malaria or was poisoned. But whatever the cause, Alexander's hours were numbered. As he lay dying in his tent, his generals gathered

Kingdom of
Antigonous

Mediterranean Sea

Alexandria

Babylon

Kingdom of
Seleucus

Kingdom of
Ptolemy

Egypt

Indus
River

Nile River

ArabianSea

Alexander's empire divided into three parts

around him, wondering who would be in command after he was gone. It was reported that when asked to whom he would leave his great empire, Alexander whispered, "to the strongest."

He died in the thirty-third year of his life. He had ruled for 13 years and amassed the largest empire the world had ever known. Like his hero Achilles, he had lived a short, glorious life that would be celebrated and remembered for all time.

Alexander's body was placed in a solid gold coffin. After a funeral in Babylon the coffin was positioned on a wagon beneath a jewel-encrusted golden temple. The wagon was drawn by 64 mules wearing golden bells across one thousand miles to Egypt. He was finally laid to rest in the city he had founded years before in the delta of the Nile, Alexandria.

After many years of struggle, Alexander's empire was finally divided among three of his generals. Seleucus ruled the Persian Empire east to the Indus River (it was called

the Seleucid empire), Antigonus gained control of Macedonia, Greece and Crete, and Ptolemy established a dynasty in Egypt.

Alexander's Legacy

Although Alexander's great empire did not hold together after his death, he did leave a rich legacy. The network of Greek cities he had established became important commercial centers. Greeks living in Europe were attracted by the trading prospects in the new cities and they flocked to inhabit them, taking their rich culture with them. Alexander had created a uniform coinage in his empire, and this greatly facilitated trade throughout the Mediterranean world. The Greek language was spoken by educated people in the major cities of his empire (the dialect spoken in Asia was called Koine); even the Christian Bible would be written in Greek. But perhaps Alexander's greatest legacy was that he had broken down many of the barriers between the East and the West and opened up the possibility a multinational sharing of trade, art and political ideals.

Questions

1. How did Philip improve his army?

2. Who was Alexander's great hero?

3. How did Alexander tame Bucephalus?

4. How did most Greeks react to the news of Philip's death?

5. Why did Alexander win at Granicus?

6. What does it mean to "untie the Gordian Knot?"

7. Describe the physique and personality of Darius the Great.

8. Why did Alexander conquer the ports along the western coast of Asia?

9. How did Alexander show his respect for foreign cultures when he was in Egypt?

10. What was Darius' "lethal weapon" at Issus?

11. Why did Alexander's men become uneasy?

12. Why did Alexander restore to Porus his kingdom?

13. Why was the return from India to Babylon so difficult for Alexander and his men?

14. To whom did Alexander leave his empire?

15. What was Alexander's legacy?

Further Thoughts

1. Demosthenes was a great orator who tried in vain to warn his fellow Athenians about the danger posed by Philip of Macedonia. He wrote a series of speeches called The Philippics, warning that an invasion by Philip would mark the end of democracy. The one time he managed to unite Athens and Thebes against Philip, the Greeks lost to the Macedonians at the battle of Chaeronea. After Philip's death, Demosthenes spoke just as fervently about the danger that Alexander presented. Some people heeded his words, but in general his pleas fell upon deaf ears. Later, when the Macedonians conquered Greece and demanded the execution of Demosthenes, the poor man ended his life by drinking poison.

2. Alexander sought out the famous philosopher Diogenes when he visited Corinth. This highly respected but eccentric philosopher believed that one should separate himself from all unnecessary luxury, and so he lived in a huge barrel, and he carried a lighted lantern by daylight in a never-ending search for an honest man. Diogenes believed in the community of mankind and opposed the idea of independent city-states. In fact, he invented the word cosmolite which meant "citizen of the world." Perhaps it was he who planted in the young conqueror's mind the idea of a world community. When Alexander came upon Diogenes he asked him if he had anything to say to him. The philosopher replied, "I would ask you to stand out of my light." Alexander, impressed with the confidence and independence of the old man, exclaimed, "If I were not Alexander, I would be Diogenes!"

3. Some Greek historians wrote that Diogenes died at the age of ninety on the very same day as Alexander, although modern scholars suspect that this

coincidence might have been contrived by romantic writers of the past.

4. Alexander had been hunting Darius when he came across the dead body of the Great King. He threw his cloak over the corpse and sent it back to Persepolis for a royal burial. He did not admire Darius the man, but he greatly respected the traditions of the Persian people.

5. Alexander outgrew the political ideas of his teacher Aristotle. While the old philosopher believed that the city-state must be a self-sufficient unit of civilization, Alexander sought a more open world-wide community. Perhaps it was in part this belief in the autonomy of each city-state that prevented Greece from evolving beyond the Golden Age. Direct democracy worked well in a city-state of 20,000 people, but the Greeks never carried the idea a step further to representative democracy. Had they done so, perhaps Greece could have expanded into the kind of multinational nation that Alexander envisioned.

6. Alexander's great military successes were due in part to his imaginative strategies. Once, when he encountered a very superstitious tribe in Illyria, he ordered his troops to march in precision in absolute silence. Ordinarily, the soldiers sang a war song and marched to the sounds of a double flute. The effect was so eerie that many enemy soldiers dashed off the battlefield in sheer fright.

Projects

1. It has been said that Alexander embodied the Greek ideal of living life to its fullest. What sacrifices do you think he made because of his love of action? Do you consider his life a full life? Why or why not? What about the Greek motto, "Nothing in excess" and the stories about the dangers of hubris? Write a short essay expressing your opinion.

2. Find out more about Demosthenes. What did he do to get over his stuttering? Write a short report about this great orator who overcame his physical limitations.

3. Make a timeline showing Alexander's accomplishments.

4. "Alexander was Achilles." Write a short essay explaining why you agree with this statement, or why you don't.

5. The Persian Empire was established by King Cyrus I (Cyrus the Great). He was one of Alexander's heroes. Find out more about Cyrus. Then write an essay, explaining why you think Alexander was drawn to him.

As we know, the Greeks called themselves Hellenes, and so the culture that Alexander helped to spread throughout western Asia and Egypt is called Hellenistic (Greek-like).

CHAPTER 17

THE HELLENISTIC AGE

Those Greeks from the mainland who rushed eastward to take advantage of the trading opportunities in Alexander's new cities strengthened the cultural traditions that had originally been established there by men recruited from Alexander's army. Each city was modeled upon Athens and contained pillared temples and government buildings, an open-air theater, gymnasiums, and a centrally located agora. The architecture was somewhat more ornate than that of the Golden Age, and elaborate Corinthian columns supported the roofs of the buildings.

A Hellenistic city had a democratic government and observed the traditional Greek religious festivals, but its citizens were also greatly influenced by the cultures of the surrounding areas as well as the new ideas and technologies emanating from the distant Orient. For this reason, the Hellenistic Age that followed Alexander's death can best be described as a blending of Greek and eastern cultures. It lasted for about three hundred years and ended when Augustus became Emperor of Rome.

Alexandria

Alexander had hoped that the city he founded in Egypt would become an international center. During the Hellenistic Age it did become the hub of trade and learning in the Mediterranean world. Although over one half of the city's population was Greek, there were also scholars and merchants from Italy, Crete, Syria, Arabia and even India.

The city stood majestically above the waters of the Nile delta like a beacon of gleaming marble. The streets were laid out in the grid pattern that Alexander had once sketched in the sand. Within its encircling walls were a Hall of Justice, government offices, warehouses and shops, while beyond lay a hippodrome and a stadium. A canal brought water from the Nile, and clay pipes conducted it to the private homes of the wealthy.

Alexandria also had a vast library of over 700,000 volumes written on papyrus; the library was part of a huge temple dedicated to the Muses (the nine Greek goddesses believed to inspire such creative activities as poetry and music), and for this reason it was called the Museum. Scholars came there to read and discuss the great works of the age, and the Museum slowly evolved into the ancient equivalent of a modern university.

The lighthouse at Alexandria

Those who came to Alexandria to study were exempt from taxes, and in some cases the Egyptian government even provided them with a living allowance.

A huge lighthouse (called the Pharos because it was built on the island of Pharas) dominated the city's skyline. Its four hundred-foot tower was crowned by a polished steel mirror that was visible to ships thirty miles away in the Mediterranean Sea. The Pharos was such an impressive structure that it was considered one of the Seven Wonders of the Ancient World. It was destroyed by an earthquake centuries ago. Today the French word for lighthouse is "phare".

Egypt was governed in those days by the Ptolemies, the dynasty established by one of Alexander's generals. The ruling class spoke Greek, worshipped Zeus and drank imported wine rather than the local beer. Unfortunately, they also treated the native Egyptians as second-class citizens.

Mainland Greece

After the death of Alexander, Athens declined as a major trading port, but it continued to thrive as a center of study and learning, especially in the areas of philosophy and rhetoric. The other city-states of mainland Greece combined to form two leagues: the Aetolian League (cities north of the Isthmus of Corinth) and the Achaean League (the Peloponnese). Greece was now better unified than it had ever been in the past, but the days of glory were over.

Hellenistic Art

The Greek artists of the Hellenistic period found that their works were greatly in demand. The new cities in Asia needed statues for their temples, parks and private gardens. Furthermore, it became fashionable among the rich throughout the Mediterranean world to have their portraits chiseled in stone. The sculptors in Athens and other mainland cities could not keep up with the demand, and eventually factories were set up near the quarries to speed up what became the mass production of statues. Boatloads of them were then shipped to all the major ports. Lifelike statues were also molded in pottery; many of these had interchangeable heads so that a customer could order a particular facial expression and the appropriate head would be placed atop a "generic" clay body.

Most Hellenistic statues differ from the classical figures of the Golden Age. The earlier statues portray the idealized human body and create a feeling of restraint and detachment. The Hellenistic figures are

The Laocoön

more realistic, and they often depict violent emotion. Rather than sculpt a handsome young athlete, the Hellenistic artist was likely to portray a wrinkled old woman or a dying soldier. A famous statue of this period is called The Laocoön. This work graphically portrays a Trojan priest and his two sons in a final, agonizing death struggle against a huge, undulating serpent. (In Greek legend, Laocoön had warned the Trojans not to take the wooden horse into the city.)

The influence of Greek art spread as far as India, where the surviving statues of Buddha that were sculpted at this time bear a striking resemblance to Apollo.

Although all the statues that have survived since the days of ancient Greece have no color beyond that of the marble itself, it is important to know that the Greek sculptors usually painted their statues to make them seem more lifelike, and sometimes they even adorned them with jewelry, such as necklaces, bracelets, earrings, and crowns. While all traces of the paint have disappeared over the centuries, there are small holes on many of the statues where the jewelry would have been attached.

Mystical Religions

The Greeks who lived in Alexander's new cities continued to worship the Olympian gods and to participate in the religious festivals. Yet, their exposure to the religions of the East made them increasingly aware of the limitations of the old Greek religion. We learned earlier that there was no moral code connected with the worship of the Olympian gods and goddesses. One of the major functions of religious traditional activities had been to bring the people together, and the sacrifices were offered to obtain favors from particular deities. But the Greek religion offered little inspiration to the people to lead a better life, nor did it fully address the important issues of sin, personal redemption, and immortality.

Some Greeks who sought a more mystical religious experience had been drawn to the cults associated with certain gods. The mystery cult of Eleusis, for example, evolved from a worship of the goddess Demeter and her daughter Persephone. It focused upon the natural cycle of the growing season, and implied that, like the farmer's crops, a human life could be reborn in another world. Members of the cult had to pass special tests before being accepted, and then they were sworn to secrecy, so we know little about their activities. We do know that they experienced a feeling of communication with the deities through highly emotional mass rituals.

During the Hellenistic Age the need for a mystical experience was often fulfilled by the religions that had flourished for centuries in the lands conquered by Alexander. The Egyptian goddess Isis appealed to many Greek women, and the Persian god Mithras was a popular deity among soldiers. In Alexandria a new god known as Serapis was invented by Ptolemy. Serapis embodied elements of the Egyptian god Osiris and the Greek gods Zeus, Apollo, and Hades. He promised virtuous people eternal life.

The Greek Language and Literature

Greek became the international language of diplomacy, literature and science throughout Alexander's former empire.

Centuries later the New Testament of the Bible would be written in Greek.

The colorful gods and goddesses of Mt. Olympus lived on in art, drama and poetry written during this period, but nature was also the subject of many important works. Theocritus, a Greek who lived for some time in Alexandria, wrote beautiful poems about the simple country life of Arcadia. Meleager wrote fascinating epigrams and inspiring love poems. Both Theocritus and Meleager had a strong influence upon later Roman and British poets. But perhaps the greatest achievements of the Hellenistic Age were in science and mathematics. You'll learn about these in the next chapter.

Questions

1. What does "Hellenistic" mean?
2. How did the Greeks living in Alexandria treat the Egyptians?
3. What was the Museum?
4. How did the Greek art of the Hellenistic Period differ from that of the Golden Age?
5. Why did foreign religious cults appeal to many Greeks?
6. Who was Theocritus?

Further Thoughts

1. Although Alexandria was a center for scholars during the Hellenistic period, Athens never lost her reputation as a place of learning. Aristotle's school, the Lyceum, continued to thrive for a century after his death. Many of the leading families of Egypt, Asia and later Rome sent their children to Athens to be educated.

2. Greek and Latin were the common languages of scholars of all nations until quite recently. And think about the names of such categories as the species of plants and animals, chemical elements and compounds, and the medicines on the shelf in the neighborhood drugstore. In the scientific community, Greek and Latin words still form the basis of a universal language.

Projects

1. Find a detailed description of Alexandria in a book or an online article. Using clay or paper mache, make a diorama of the city. Include such structures as the lighthouse, museum, and hippodrome, and show the grid pattern of the streets.

2. Find a book about ancient and classical art in your library. Then select two Greek statues that are shown in the book, one that was made during the Golden Age and one dating from the Hellenistic Age. Study the pictures carefully, and read any text that concerns them. Then write a short report comparing and contrasting the two statues. Be sure to tell which statue you prefer (and why).

The Winged Victory of Samothrace

3.   The Winged victory of Samothrace is a marble statue of Nike, the Greek goddess of victory. It was made in the second century B.C.E. Despite her missing head, this is one of the most famous sculptures in the world. It can be seen at the Louvre Museum in Paris. Search the Internet to learn more about this statue. Find out where it was made, when and how it was rediscovered, what happened to it during World War II, and what is so special about its appearance. Describe your findings in a report.

4.   The Venus de Milo is another very famous Greek statue dating from the Hellenistic period. (Venus is the Roman name for Aphrodite.) The twisting motion of the figure is very typical of statues made at this time. Find out more about this statue and write a short report.

5.   Who were the nine Greek muses? Find out and then make a list, giving their names, their special domains (area of influence, such as music or poetry), and their emblems (such as a lyre or writing tablet). What does the word "muse" mean today?

The Venus de Milo

Thalia, the muse of comedy

CHAPTER 18

ADVANCES IN SCIENCE

As a race, the Greeks were extremely inquisitive about the make-up and functioning of the natural world, but the greatest advances in scientific knowledge were made beyond the shores of the mainland in the Aegean islands, Ionia, southern Italy, and, of course, Alexandria. It was in those bustling trading centers that ideas as well as products were constantly exchanged, and the scholars living there were able to freely embrace new concepts and then use them to make dramatic discoveries of their own.

Thales of Miletus

Thales of Miletus was the first great Greek philosopher. He lived in the seventh century B.C.E. in the Ionian sea-port that was later destroyed by the Persians. Remember, the word "philosopher" originally referred to anyone who enjoyed studying things. Thales was primarily interested in astronomy and mathematics, and his curiosity about the measurement of distances took him to Egypt. There he studied the structures of the pyramids and thought about the rules of geometry that had been applied to build them. He noticed that at a certain time of day a man's shadow is equal to his height, and he used this principle to measure the height of the Great Pyramid.

Thales also studied eclipses of the sun, and according to legend he even predicted one successfully. He was greatly impressed by the relatively efficient 365-day calendar used by the Egyptians, and he introduced it to the Greeks. Our own calendar is based upon it.

Thales' most important contribution to science was his theory that the world had been formed by a natural process and was not the creation of the gods. Furthermore, he proposed that nature was governed by certain unchanging laws, and he said that human beings could discover these laws by carefully observing their environment. Thales was the first Greek to write about the science of nature (*physis*), and his attempt to understand and explain the origin of life using scientific rather than religious evidence marked an important break with the past. Small wonder that Aristotle regarded him as his spiritual mentor.

Other New Theories

Anaximander was a pupil of Thales. After years of studying the heavens, he concluded that the earth had been produced by a huge explosion. He also proposed that the sun, moon and stars moved in circles around the earth, a theory that would be supported by most scientists for two millennia. Anaximander observed the creatures of the earth, and he concluded that the first living things lived in the water and that over time some of these creatures learned to live on the land. It was from them that human beings evolved. His theory seemed to be confirmed when a later scholar, Xenophanes, examined some fossils and decided that they were the remains of plants and animals that had lived millions of years ago preserved in rock.

These observations, made over 2,000 years ago, form the basis of the modern science of evolution.

Anaximander also drew the earliest known map of the world upon a brass tablet. Not surprisingly, Greece lies in the center of the map, attached to the rest of Europe and separated by the sea from Asia. Of course, the land is entirely surrounded by water (Ocean). In the sixth century B.C.E. Hecataeus revised the world map to include northern Africa (which he labeled as part of Asia).

Other Greek scholars tried to ascertain the basic components of the universe. And what was the single substance from which everything else had evolved? Was it liquid or gas? Scientific investigation was in its infancy at this time, and yet revolutionary discoveries did take place. An Ionian named Democritus came to the conclusion that all things are made up of tiny particles called atoms, an amazingly accurate deduction in a time when there were no scientific instruments.

Pythagoras

Pythagoras was a philosopher born near Miletus who traveled extensively in Europe, Asia and Africa and then settled in Crotona, a Greek colony in southern Italy. There he founded a school to study geometry, arithmetic, astronomy and music. His school accepted women students as well as men—an astonishing innovation in the strongly male-oriented Greek society.

Pythagoras knew something about right triangles from a rule of geometry that the Egyptians had used to make the corners of their buildings square. According to this rule, if a triangle has sides which are three, four

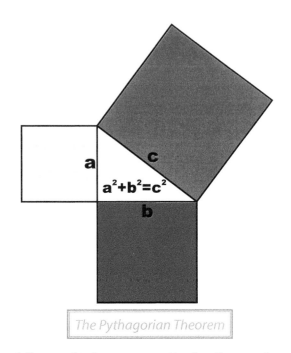

The Pythagorian Theorem

and five units long respectively, the angle between the two shorter sides is a right angle (90 degrees). Pythagoras used this knowledge to make a new rule: in a right triangle the area of the square on the longest side equals the sum of the areas (squares) of the other two sides. This is called the Pythagrian Theorem, and it is one of the basic rules of modern geometry. He also discovered that the sum of the angles within any triangle equals two right angles.

Pythagoras believed that ours is an orderly universe whose center is the earth. He was the first person to call the earth round and to refer to the universe as cosmos (a Greek word meaning order). He loved mathematics and proposed that the arrangement of the universe could be expressed in numbers. He later experimented with music and discovered the numerical ratio between the length of the string of an instrument and the note it produces. A shorter string produces a higher pitch than a longer one. He also observed that the sounds produced by different strings are especially harmonious when the lengths of the strings are in a certain numerical proportion to one another, such as three to two or four to five. Based upon his findings Pythagoras created a seven note musical scale. Despite their great strides in scientific discovery, the Greeks remained a superstitious people. Pythagoras himself believed in reincarnation (the concept that the soul of a dead person was passed on to the body of another creature in which it was reborn). He told his students that he could clearly remember his own past lives, including the time he fought in the Trojan War.

The Heliocentric Theory

Anaxagoras was the teacher of Pericles and later (possibly) Socrates. He proposed that the moon did not produce its own light, but rather that it reflected the light of the sun. He wrote that the sun was a red hot stone "considerably larger than the Peloponnese." Like Thales, he studied eclipses, and he proposed that they were caused by the moon passing between the earth and the sun, blocking the light.

Aristarchus was an astronomer who was educated at Aristotle's Lyceum. He accurately measured the size of the sun and the moon, and he calculated their distance from earth. His estimate of the length of a year (the time it takes the earth to circle the sun) was only 7 minutes and 16 seconds too short. He argued against Aristotle's view that the earth is the center of the universe, instead proposing that the moon, earth and planets move around the sun. This is called the heliocentric theory. Unfortunately, the people of the ancient world were accustomed to the belief that the earth was the center of all things, and they scoffed at his idea that our planet was but

one of many heavenly bodies circling the sun. The heliocentric theory would not be accepted by the scientific community until the sixteenth century C.E.

Aristotle

We have already learned about Aristotle's accomplishments in the field of science. He was one of the earliest proponents of the scientific method: he closely observed an aspect of the natural world, analyzed his findings and then carefully recorded his conclusions. He classified over five hundred animals, and he was the first to observe that dolphins were not fish but mammals because they give birth to live offspring. Aristotle also studied the development of chick embryos and drew detailed charts documenting the changes that occurred. (He preserved the embryos in honey.)

Aristotle's work in natural science was carried on by Theophrastus, who later became the head of the Lyceum. Theophrastus analyzed the specimens and data made available by Alexander during his marches through Asia. After his death, the focus of scientific research would move from Athens to Alexandria.

Advances of the Hellenistic Age

The Hellenistic Age marked the high point of scientific research and discovery in the ancient world. The surge of intellectual activity was spurred on by the common language spoken throughout Alexander's empire that enabled scholars of different cultures to share their knowledge. Another contributing factor was the weakening of traditional religious beliefs.

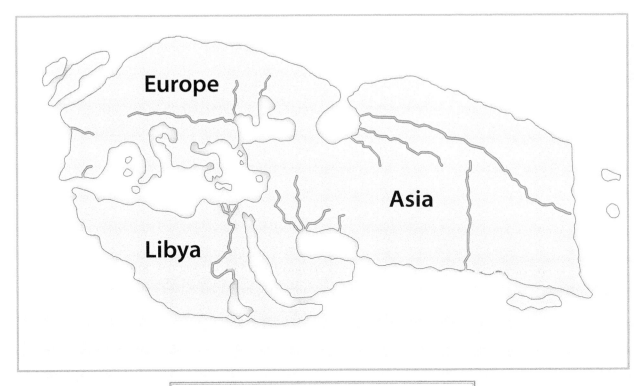

The world according to Eratosthenes (c. 226 B.C.E.)

One of the great mathematicians of the time was a Greek named Euclid who founded a school in Alexandria. He wrote a series of textbooks (*The Elements*) which describe the specific steps that must be followed to solve different kinds of problems in geometry. Euclid is called the Father of Geometry and his works form the basis of modern geometry texts.

Eratosthenes was the chief librarian of the Museum at Alexandria. In his book about geography he described the world as a sphere. His estimate of the circumference of the earth was nearly accurate (it was off by only 200 miles). He proposed that by sailing west from Spain a ship would eventually arrive in India "if there is no large land mass in the way"—this theory was not put to the test until the time of Christopher Columbus!

In the second century B.C.E. the astronomer Hipparchus of Rhodes (an island off the coast of Ionia) drew a grid of lines on a map of the surface of the earth which were the forerunners of our lines of latitude and longitude. He also charted hundreds of stars.

Occasionally, science took a few steps backwards. Ptolemy (no relation to Alexander's general) studied astronomy in Alexandria in the first century C.E. He wrote a book that described and catalogued the findings of the more important Greek astronomers living from the fifth century B.C.E. to his own day. Ptolemy refuted the heliocentric theory of Aristarchus and confidently confirmed that the earth was a stationary object encircled by the sun, moon and stars. To his credit, however, is an eight-volume book on geography listing all the known places on the earth and arranging them according to longitude and latitude.

Eureka!

Archimedes is often considered the greatest mathematician of ancient times. He settled in Syracuse (Sicily) after studying in Alexandria. His work in geometry focused primarily on the areas and volumes of curved surfaces. He is well known for his accurate calculation of the ratio of the circumference of a circle to its diameter (called pi). Today middle school students are able to solve their homework problems in geometry because of Archimedes' famous formula.

This imaginative Greek also gained renown for his theory concerning the mass of a body immersed in a liquid. There is a well-known story about how he made his discovery. King Hieron of Syracuse once ordered a crown of gold, but he was worried that not all the gold had been used in the finished product. He therefore asked Archimedes, who had a reputation for being very knowledgeable about scientific matters, to find a means of determining whether he had been cheated by the metal smith who made the crown. Had the smith melted down a smaller proportion of gold allotted for the crown than he should have, replacing some of the precious metal with silver? Archimedes wondered how he could discover the amount of gold used, but he was baffled.

Later, as he stepped into his bath, the ever-curious mathematician observed the amount of water that spilled over the rim of the tub when he sat down. He estimated that it was equal to the space taken up by his own body in the bath waters. He also noticed that the water overflowed less when he was submerged. On the spot he formulated a rule about water displacement known as Archimedes' Principle: a submerged body displaces an amount of water equal to its volume (density). According to legend, when Archimedes realized he could apply his new-found knowledge to solve the problem of the crown he jumped out of the tub and ran naked through the streets shouting, "Eureka!" (I've found it!).

Soon afterwards, he used his principle to determine the amount of gold in the crown. He knew that a certain weight of silver had more volume (was denser) than a similar weight of gold. Therefore, according to his principle, the silver should displace more water than a similar weight of gold. When Archimedes submerged the crown in a basin, he noticed that it did indeed displace more water than a golden bar of the same weight. The smith had cheated the king.

Archimedes had a number of practical inventions. One was the water screw, a device used to pump water into irrigation ditches and out of flooded mines. It is still used in developing countries today. He also wrote a detailed explanation of the function of a lever.

The displacement of water in the tub

The Medical Advances of Hippocrates

At first the Greeks believed that disease was caused by the anger of the gods, and the early Greek doctors were the priests of Asclepius, the god of healing. When a person became ill, he went to a temple of Asclepius and made a sacrifice. Afterwards the temple priests offered him medicines (few of which worked) and magical charms. In many cases a "patient" was allowed to spend the night at the temple, sleeping on the skins of sacrificed animals. If he was lucky, Asclepius would magically appear in a dream and tell him how he could be cured. Actually, a priest impersonated the god, but the power of suggestion often made the patient believe that he would recover. Many maladies are aggravated by tension and worry, and so by helping the person to relax the priest could relieve any discomfort that was caused by anxiety. People who were seriously ill, of course, would find no cure for their sufferings at the temple.

Hippocrates, who lived in the fourth century B.C.E., was a scientist who sought to separate the practice of medicine from religious beliefs. He studied the symptoms of his patients and looked for a physical cause for their afflictions. He experimented with various herbal medications, carefully monitoring their effects. He kept a detailed record of his patients' progress and used the data to help other people suffering from similar diseases. He came to the conclusion that a sound diet, proper hygiene and rest were essential for recuperation. They also were the keys to good health.

Hippocrates created a school of medicine on the island of Kos, and he established high ethical standards for his students. He believed that a doctor should be honest with his patient and keep matters pertaining to his case confidential; furthermore, he should do everything possible to protect and preserve human life. These ideals are embodied in the Hippocratic Oath (see Appendix), a professional creed that was administered to young doctors until quite recently. Today many medical schools are using alternative oaths, because they consider some of the premises of Hippocrates outdated.

Other Studies of Human Anatomy

In the third century B.C.E. Greek scientists in Alexandria were fascinated by the discoveries made by Egyptians in the preparation of mummies, and they began to dissect and study the bodies of deceased human beings. Herophilus identified the major organs, and he discovered the difference between veins and arteries. His greatest contribution to medicine was his discovery that the brain is the center of the nervous system (the Egyptians had thought that the center of thought and emotion was the heart).

Many of the scientific discoveries of the Hellenistic period took place in newly built centers of research where Greeks interacted with scholars from other cultures. They were to have a profound influence on the development of science in the following centuries. Alexander would have been pleased.

Questions

1. Why did most scientific discoveries take place beyond the mainland of Greece?

2. What was Thales' most important contribution to science?

3. What was Democritus' theory of the composition of matter?

4. What is the Pythagorean Theorem?

5. On what issue did Aristarchus disagree with his mentor, Aristotle?

6. What discovery caused Archimedes to leap from the bathtub in delight?

7. Who was Asclepius?

8. What is the Hippocratic Oath?

Further Thoughts

1. Asclepius was the son of Apollo. He was brought up by a centaur (a creature that was half man, half horse) who taught him about medicine. Athena gave the young Asclepius two bottles of magic blood: the blood in one bottle would kill anything, while that in the other could bring the dead back to life. As it turned out, Asclepius frequently used the second bottle and brought so many people back to life that Hades complained to Zeus. "The land of the dead was becoming over-populated!" Zeus killed Asclepius with a thunderbolt (he was only a demi-god and so he was mortal), but the Olympian later changed his mind and restored Asclepius to life, making him an immortal god.

2. Asclepius' daughter Hygeia became the goddess of health, and she is the source of our word "hygiene." His other daughter was Panacea (today a panacea is a "cure-all" medicine).

3. Statues of Asclepius often show him holding a snake (a symbol of regeneration). A snake-entwined staff, called the caduceus, is the symbol of the modern medical profession.

4. Galen was a Greek surgeon living in Rome in the second century C.E. who had studied in Alexandria. He discovered that blood flows through the arteries (earlier scientists had thought that air flowed through them) and his work led to an understanding of how blood circulates throughout the human body.

Statue of Asclepius

5. The Greeks had tax-financed medical treatment. This was the world's first medicare.

6. Despite the advances made in medicine, many people continued to rely upon superstition and magic when they were ill or wounded. Common remedies of the Hellenistic Age included the following: for a fever, swallow the blood from the ear of an ass, or else the liver of a cat that was killed when the moon was waning; for a broken bone, apply the ashes of a pig's jaw; for a broken rib, apply the dung of a goat mixed with old wine.

A caduceus

7. Aspirin dates back to the ancient Greeks. Hippocrates noted that a brew of willow leaves, which contain salicin (an ingredient of aspirin), was helpful as a pain-killer in childbirth. (Salix is the Latin name for willow.)

Salix willow

Projects

1. Thales of Miletus was often taunted by his neighbors who thought he was too intellectual. In order to show that he had a practical side, he studied the climate of the island of Lesbor and determined that there would be a bumper crop of olives that season. Then he bought up all the local olive presses! How did this prove that his head was not "in the clouds"? What did he gain from his action?

2. Draw a right triangle of any dimension. Then test the Pythagorian theorem (the square of the longest side of a right triangle equals the squares of the other two sides). Does it work? If not, try again!

3. Ptolemy proposed a geocentric theory of the universe. Using your knowledge of Greek roots and the information you've read about Ptolemy, define the word "geocentric."

4. Life at Pythagoras' school was spartan, to say the least. Find out more about the strict rules regarding food, drink and morals, and write a short report.

5. Read the Hippocratic Oath in the Appendix. Which ideas are still valuable and meaningful in today's world? Which sections of the oath seem out-dated?

Relief statue of Achilles

EPILOGUE

The Romans conquered Greece in the second century B.C.E. and made it a province of their own rapidly expanding empire. Over the next 100 years Roman legions gradually subdued the armies of all the nations surrounding the Mediterranean, which they arrogantly referred to as "our sea" (*Mare Nostrum*).

There was a great difference between the highly sophisticated Greeks and their brash, militaristic overlords. Fortunately, the Romans appreciated and valued the rich civilization of the people they had conquered, and they made great efforts to assimilate many aspects of it into their own more primitive culture. In fact, they sent their own children to Athens to receive their formal education. Later, the Roman scholar Horace would write, "Greece the captive enthralled her savage captor!" The Olympian gods were given Roman names and credentials, the life-like Hellenic statues were copied by Italian sculptors, and the theories and principles formulated by Greek scientists were applied to produce great feats of Roman engineering. Greek poets from Homer to Meleager inspired Roman writers, and they in turn would greatly influence later English bards.

In their new role as teachers of the nation that had conquered them, the Greeks were able to perpetuate much of the extraordinary civilization we have been studying. At the same time, their way of life was brought by the Romans to societies in Africa and Europe that had not previously been touched by Alexander.

Our debt to the Greeks is immeasurable. As we conclude our study of their ancient culture, let's take time to consider what made this people unique among the early inhabitants of the Mediterranean world. What special qualities enabled them to achieve such incredible heights in a relatively short period of time? Optimism, of course, and a lively curiosity are characteristics that immediately spring to mind. And the Greeks were certainly resourceful. The early farmers had to work hard to scratch out a living on their rocky peninsula, each man depending upon his various abilities to support himself and his family. From this humble beginning evolved the Greek ideal of competency in many aspects of life, but "nothing in excess."

Dionysus

Pride in their accomplishments led the Greeks to create a family of gods modeled upon the human race. Their gentle mockery of the human-like weaknesses of the Olympians was, perhaps, their way of laughing at themselves. Such irreverence was not seen in other parts of the ancient world. Indeed, the Babylonians lay prostrate upon the ground before statues of their god Marduk, and the Egyptians devoted their lives to serving their god-kings, the pharaohs. The colorful figures of Greek mythology have entertained audiences for over two thousand years, and the lessons that they teach are timeless.

The Greeks knew that a meaningful life began with an understanding of one's self, and generations of poets and philosophers thoroughly explored the complexities of human desires and emotions. A firm belief in the worth of the individual led logically to a love of individual freedom. While other peoples were ruled by absolute monarchs, Athenian citizens considered personal liberty a birthright. Laws had been formulated and written down by earlier societies, but the Greeks were the first to devise a form of government that catered to the needs of the common people. Ironically, the Greek city-states cherished their freedom so much they were never able to be effectively united as a single nation except in times of war.

While their civilization flourished, the Greeks' celebration of the human potential knew no bounds. They were convinced that man, with his superior intellect, could create order out of the chaos of nature, just as he had established a harmonious society within his own species. "Man is the measure of all things," said the philosopher Protagoras, taking this confidence in human endeavor a step further by implying that the objects of the physical world existed according to how man perceived them.

The Greek spirit is still very much alive today. That ancient standard of self-mastery, intellectual curiosity, and quiet courage during difficult times remains the mark of a highly civilized man, a person of "class." And think about those imaginative people of the ancient world the next time you see a graceful pillar, listen to a congressman on television, attend a play, compete in a footrace, recognize the symbol for FTD florists (that's Hermes, of course!), admire a statue, solve a problem in geometry, perform the labors of Heracles in a video game, or simply marvel at the achievements of mankind. After all these years, Greek aspirations and accomplishments remain a vital part of the modern age.

Hermes, messenger of the gods

Projects

1.   Make a collage. Using five or six magazines, look for pictures or words that seem to have something to do with ancient Greece. These can include a picture of a beautiful woman that reminds you of Aphrodite or Helen, a photograph of a house with pillars, a Ford Taurus (remember the Minotaur?), an athlete in action, or a word (such as psychology) that has Greek roots. Be imaginative! Cut out the pictures (and words) you select and glue them on a piece of poster board.

2.   Write a newspaper. This is a group project. Select a period or event in Greek history, such as the Persian Wars or the death of Socrates. Then think of the general areas that are covered in daily newspapers: headlines, sports, gossip column, local events, entertainment, books, and don't forget advertising. Political cartoons are always an asset. Decide on a name for your newspaper (the Theban Times, the Athenian Herald, etc.). Assign each member of the group to cover one area. Once the articles and illustrations have been drafted, plan your layout. Cut and paste onto a new document until you have your page (or pages) arranged to your satisfaction, and then print out copies of your newspaper of ancient Greece. Hand them out to your classmates and wait for the rave reviews!

3.   Make a list of the ways that the civilization of ancient Greece continues to influence the modern world.

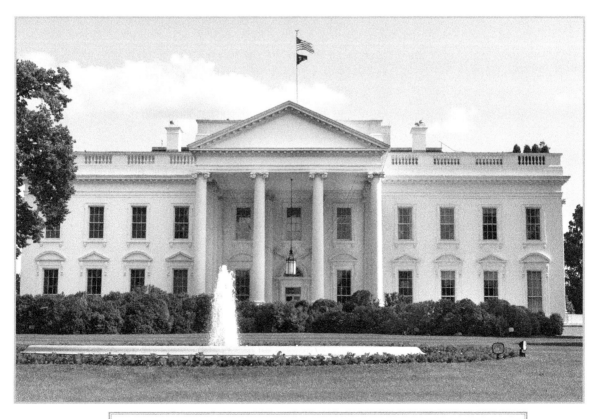

Greek pillars and pediment grace the White House, Washington, DC

Timeline of Major Events

Neolithic Period

c. 4000 B.C.E.	Crete is settled

Bronze Age

c. 2000 B.C.E.	The Acheans enter Greece
c. 1600-1450	Height of Minoan civilization
c. 1600-1100 B.C.E.	The Mycenean Age
c. 1200 B.C.E.	The fall of Troy
1140 B.C.E.	The Dorian invasion

Dark Ages

776 B.C.E.	The first Olympic Games

Archaic Period

c. 750 B.C.E.	Homer
c. 720 B.C.E.	Greek first alphabet in use
594 B.C.E.	Solon's Reforms
490-479 B.C.E.	The Persian Wars

Classical Period

460-429 B.C.E.	The Age of Pericles
431-404 B.C.E.	The Peloponnesian War
399 B.C.E.	Death of Socrates
336-323 B.C.E.	Era of Alexander the Great

Hellenistic Period

323-30 B.C.E.	Alexandria becomes a great center of learning. Greek culture spreads to Asia and Africa

Note: In the timeline c. is used to denote approximate dates. It comes from the Latin word "circa" which means "around." So c. 800 B.C.E. means around or approximately 800 B.C.E.

APPENDIX

Speech of Pericles on the Occasion of the Funeral of Athenian Soldiers Killed During the Peloponnesian War (excerpts)

I will not talk about the battles we have won. I will not talk about how our ancestors became great. Instead, I will talk about our spirit and our way of life. I will talk about those things that have made us great.

Our government does not copy those of our neighbors. Instead, ours is a model for them. Ours is a democracy. The power is in the hands of the people. It is not in the hands of a small group. Everyone is equal before the law. We do not care what class a man belongs to. We care only about his ability. No one is kept from taking part in government because he is poor.

Our political life is free and open. So is our day-to-day life. We do not care if our neighbors enjoy themselves in their own way. We are free and tolerant. But in public affairs we obey the laws. We especially obey the ones that protect the lowly.

Here is another point. When our work is done, we enjoy our free time. There are ceremonies and contests all year. In our homes there is beauty and taste. Our city brings us good things from all over the world.

And our city is open to the whole world. We never keep people out for fear they will spy on us. We have no secrets. We do not rely on trickery. We rely on our own hearts and hands. We are brave in facing danger. Our love of beauty does not lead to weakness. Our love of mind does not make us soft.

Everyone here is interested in the *polis*. We do not say those who are not interested in politics are minding their own business. We say they have no business here at all!

Looking at everything, I say Athens is a school for the whole of Greece. Future ages will wonder at us. The present age wonders at us now. Everywhere we have left memorials of our greatness. For this great city of ours, these men fought and died. Each of us who still lives should gladly work for our great city.

I could tell you what we gain by defeating our enemies. Instead, I would rather have you gaze on Athens' greatness every day. Then you would fall in love with our city. You would realize Athens' greatness.

Make up your minds to this. Our happiness depends on our freedom. And our freedom depends on our courage. Because of that, I will not mourn the dead. In their lives, happiness and death went hand in hand.

Abraham Lincoln's Gettysburg Address

Fourscore and seven years ago our fathers brought forth on this continent a new nation, conceived in liberty and dedicated to the proposition that all men are created equal. Now we are engaged in a great civil war, testing whether that nation or any nation so conceived and so dedicated can long endure. We are met on a great battlefield of that war. We have come to dedicate a portion of that field as a final resting-place for those who here gave their lives that that nation might live. It is altogether fitting and proper that we should do this. But in a larger sense, we cannot dedicate, we cannot consecrate, we cannot hallow this ground. The brave men, living and dead, who struggled here have consecrated it far above our poor power to add or detract. The world will little note nor long remember what we say here, but it can never forget what they did here. It is for us, the living, rather to be dedicated here to the unfinished work which they who fought here have thus far so nobly advanced. It is rather for us to be here dedicated to the great task remaining before us—that from these honored dead we take increased devotion to that cause for which they gave the last full measure of devotion—that we here highly resolve that these dead shall not have died in vain, that this nation under God shall have a new birth of freedom, and that government of the people, by the people, and for the people shall not perish from the earth.

The Hippocratic Oath

I swear by Apollo the physician and Aesclepius and health and all-heal and all the gods and goddesses that according to my ability and judgment I will keep this oath and this stipulation: to reckon him who taught me this art equally dear to me as my parents, to share my substance with him and relieve his necessities, if required, to look upon his offspring in the same footing as my own brothers and to teach them his art if they shall wish to learn it without fee or stipulation and that by precept, lecture, and every other mode of instruction I will impart a knowledge of the art to my own sons and those of my teachers and to disciples bound by a stipulation and oath according to the law of medicine, but none to others.

I will follow that system of regimen which, according to my ability and judgment, I consider for the benefit of my patients, and abstain from whatever is deleterious and mischievous. I will give no deadly medicine to any one if asked nor suggest any such counsel, and in like manner I will not give to a woman a pessary to produce abortion. With purity and with holiness I will pass my life and practice my art, I will not cut persons laboring under the stone but will leave this to be done by men who are practitioners of this work. Into whatever houses I enter, I will go into them for the benefit of the sick and will abstain from every voluntary act of mischief and corruption, and further, from the seduction of females or males, of freemen and slaves. Whatever, in connection with my professional practice, or not in connection with it, I see or hear, in the life of men, which ought not to be spoken of abroad, I will not divulge as reckoning that all such should be kept secret.

While I continue to keep this oath unviolated, may it be granted to me to enjoy life and the practice of the art, respected by all men, in all times, but should I trespass and violate this oath, may the reverse be my lot.

Guide to Pronunciation

Achaean — a-ke´an

Achilles — a-kil´ez

Acropolis — a-cro´po-lis

Aegean — e-je´an

Aeschylus — es´-ki-lus

agora — ag´o-ra

Alcibiades — al-si-bi´i-dez

Anatolia — an-atol´ia

Anaxagoras — an-aks-ag´o-ras

Anaximander — a-nak-si-man´der

Aphrodite — a-fro-di´te

Apollo — a-pol´o

Archimedes — ar-ki-me´dez

archon — ar´kon

arete — a-re´te

Aristarchus — ar-is-tar´kus

Aristophanes — ar-is-tof´a-nez

Aristotle — ar-is-to´tul

Boeotia — be-o´sha

Bucephalus — bu-sef´a-lus

Cerberus — ser´ber-us

Charon — kar´on

chiton — ki´ton

Cleisthenes — klis´the-nez

Cronus — kro´nus

Cyrus — si´rus

Darius — dar-i´us

Delphi — del´fi

Delos — de´los

Draco — dra´ko

Ecclesia — e-kle´si-a

Eratosthenes — er-a-tos´the-nez

Euboea — u-be´a

Euclid — u´klid

Euripides — u-rip´i-dez

Pheidippides — fih-dip´i-dez

Gaea — je´a

Hephaestus — he-fes´tus

Herodotus — her-od´o-tus

Hippocrates — hi-pok´ra-tez

Iliad — il´i-ad

Ionia — i-on´ia

Iphegenia — i-fi-ga´nia

Issus — is´us

Homer — ho´mer

Knossos — nos´us

Leonidas — le-on´i-das

Lyceum — li-se´um

Lycurgus — li-ker´gus

Menelaus — men-e-la´us

Miletus — mil-e´tus

Milo — mi´lo

Miltiades — mil-te´ah-dez

Minoan — mi´no-an

Minos — mi´nos

Mycenae — mi-se´ne

Mycenaeans — mi´su-ne´uns

Odyssey — od´i-si

pancratium — pan-kra´shum

Pausanias — po-sa´ni-as

Peisistratus — pi-sis´tra-tus

Peloponnese — pel´o-po-nes´

Pericles — per´i-klez

Plato — pla´to

Pnyx — niks

polis — po´lis

Ptolemy — tol´e-mi

Pythagoras — pi-thag´o-ras

Salamis — sal´a-mis

Socrates — sok´ra-tez

Solon — so´lon

Sophocles — sof´o-klez

Thales — tha´lez

Themistocles — the-mis´to-klez

Thermopylae — ther-mo´pi-le

Thucydides — thu-sid´i-dez

Xenophon — zen´o-fon

Xerxes — zerk´sez

Zeus — zoos

Index